Engaging the Arab & Islamic Worlds through Public Diplomacy:
A Report and Action Recommendations

Engaging the Arab & Islamic Worlds through Public Diplomacy:
A Report and Action Recommendations

Edited by
William A. Rugh

Public Diplomacy Council
School of Media and Public Affairs
The George Washington University
805 21st Street, NW, Suite 400
Washington, DC 20052 USA
Telephone: 202-994-0389
E-mail: pdi410@gwu.edu
Web site: http://pdi.gwu.edu

ISBN 0-9764391-0-7

The findings, interpretations, and conclusions expressed here are those of the authors and do not necessarily reflect the views of the Public Diplomacy Council.

Contents

Acknowledgments

Our deep appreciation for their efforts goes to Ambassador William Rugh, the volume editor; to Ms. Kris Rusch, who served as the manuscript and layout editor; and to the ten other distinguished writers who contributed to this book. Together they have produced a welcome and needed look at ways the United States can and should engage the Arab and Islamic worlds. This book, a follow-on to the Public Diplomacy Council's successful forum on this subject in February 2004, goes well beyond the points and ideas raised at that event. Our hope is that this volume will provoke fresh thinking and initiatives for both the policymaker and the student of public diplomacy.

The Public Diplomacy Council wishes to recognize the generous support for this project from private foundation sources. The principal benefactor of *Engaging the Arab & Islamic Worlds Through Public Diplomacy: A Report and Action Recommendations* is the Stuart Family Foundation of Lake Forest, Illinois. Other major contributions were made by the Holden Family Foundation and the Lawrence M. Gelb Foundation in the name of the Council of American Ambassadors.

Without the generosity of these supporters, this project could not have come to fruition. On behalf of the Board and Members of the Public Diplomacy Council and of readers of this publication who will benefit from the analysis and information it offers, I offer our sincerest thanks.

McKinney H. Russell
President, The Public Diplomacy Council

Introduction

William A. Rugh

IN SEPTEMBER 2001, the American public became aware that the United States has a deadly serious problem with public opinion abroad, especially among Arabs and Muslims. Foreign sympathy for Americans swelled after the terrorist attacks but quickly dissipated in the face of pointed and substantial Arab and Muslim criticism of the United States. Now, many Americans in Congress, the media, and academe are asking if public diplomacy can help restore the American image.

Public diplomacy can be defined as informing, engaging, and influencing foreign publics in support of a country's national interests.[1] Public diplomacy professionals work towards these ends in several ways. First, they help explain to foreign audiences the rationale for the policies of the administration in office, as well as the American public's support for these policies. Second, they help these audiences understand American society and culture. Third, they provide policymakers with information about, and analysis of, foreign public opinion about U.S. interests.

Some argue that only changes in American foreign policy itself, not public diplomacy, will substantially improve the American image abroad. Public diplomacy aimed at foreign public opinion is certainly no panacea, but it is an important aspect of a successful foreign policy. As the U.S. Advisory Commission on Public Diplomacy stated in a September 2004 report, "In governments throughout the world, public opinion greatly influences the direction of policy."[2] Diplomatic, military, and economic

---

1. There are other definitions. For example, USIA sometimes included the goal of "broadening links between American individuals and institutions and their counterparts abroad." The benefits of many public diplomacy mechanisms, such as exchange programs, are not restricted to foreigners.

2. Barbara M. Barrett, et al., introduction to *2004 Report of the United States Advisory Commission on Public Diplomacy* (Washington, DC: U.S. Department of State, 2004), http://www.state.gov/r/adcompd/rls/36275.htm.

power are necessary but not sufficient to achieve U.S. goals abroad. Public diplomacy must also be enlisted in this effort. Yet, since the end of the Cold War, America has neglected to develop this crucial component.

In recent years, several organizations and study groups have published recommendations on ways to improve American public diplomacy.[3] The 9/11 Commission urged the United States to do much more to "engage in the struggle of ideas" with the Muslim world.[4] Most of those reports were written primarily from a home-based perspective, and they made recommendations that focused on public diplomacy management in the United States. They gave less attention to the actual practice of public diplomacy by seasoned American professionals.

This report takes a different approach. It offers the views of practitioners who have direct experience with public diplomacy in the Arab and Muslim worlds. While some previous studies examined aspects of field activities and made a few recommendations on operational matters,[5] this report goes further by devoting nearly all of its attention to the specific tools of public diplomacy and how they are actually being used abroad.

The authors of these essays have intimate knowledge of the Arab and Muslim worlds. Most of them are professional public diplomacy experts who know those worlds from living and working there. Most have actually used the major tools of public diplomacy, and they base their judgments on their long-term familiarity with ways to reach foreign audiences in general, and Arabs and Muslims in particular.

Shibley Telhami, a leading scholar of Middle Eastern affairs, has undertaken unique and innovative studies of Arab opinion and published important analyses of Arab-American relations. His chapter opens this volume. In the three following chapters, Kenton Keith, Barry Fulton, and James Bullock describe the changing world of the public affairs

---

3. See, for example, Peter G. Peterson, et al., *Finding America's Voice* (New York: Council on Foreign Relations, 2003); Edward P. Djerejian, *Changing Minds, Winning Peace: A New Strategic Direction for U.S. Public Diplomacy in the Arab and Muslim World*, report of the U.S. Advisory Group on Public Diplomacy for the Arab and Muslim World (Washington, DC: 2003); Stephen Johnson and Helle Dale, *How to Reinvigorate U.S. Public Diplomacy* (Washington DC: The Heritage Foundation, 2003); Georgetown University Institute for the Study of Diplomacy, *Talking with the Islamic World: Is the Message Getting Through?* (Washington DC: Georgetown University Institute for the Study of Diplomacy 2002); Hady Amr, *The Need to Communicate: How to Improve U.S. Public Diplomacy with the Islamic World* (Washington DC: The Brookings Institution, 2004).

4. National Commission on Terrorist Attacks upon the United States, *The 9/11 Commission Report*, Authorized edition (New York: W.W. Norton and company, 2004), 375–77.

5. One such study is *Changing Minds, Winning Peace*.

officer. These veteran public diplomacy professionals have for many years directed public diplomacy programs in Arab and Muslim countries and in Washington, so they are intimately familiar with how such programs actually work. Next, different views on international broadcasting are offered by Alan Heil, a long-time professional and senior official at the Voice of America; Norman Pattiz, a successful American broadcast owner and a member of the Broadcasting Board of Governors; and Marc Lynch, a scholar who has made a close study of the content of Arab broadcasting and its role in Arab society.

In the next section, Barry Ballow, who has managed global exchange programs from Washington, and Cresencio Arcos, a former foreign service officer who is currently an official at Homeland Security, present their perspectives on educational exchange programs.

Print media are then discussed and analyzed by Howard Cincotta, who has been a career professional with USIA and State, managing public diplomacy programs over a period of many years.

My final essay ties together major themes that emerge from these chapters and presents an action plan for consideration by the U.S. Administration.

The Public Diplomacy Council, a non-profit organization whose members are professionals in the field, has sponsored this report as a way of contributing to the ongoing debate in the United States about what is being done and what should be done in this essential field. New technologies, shifting international strategic positions, and new attitudes in America since 9/11 have changed public diplomacy practices. Yet, with only minor modification, many of the ideas and tools that public diplomacy experts have developed over the years could well serve the United States today. It is therefore important that we are fully aware of past and present approaches that have been field-tested and found valuable. We should not try to reinvent the wheel; rather, we should build on proven best practices for a more effective national effort. This volume is intended to advance that effort.

1. Reaching the Public in the Middle East

Shibley Telhami

America's image in the Arab world has undergone a remarkable journey over the past century. For most of the 20th century, America was seen as the champion of freedom and self-determination, the land of opportunity, a place whose standards were coveted and envied. Even today, public opinion surveys in the Arab world clearly show that majorities continue to admire many of the core values America stood for. But the magnitude of the transformation is best captured by a specific contrast: a reversal of fortune for both France and the United States in the Middle East over the past century.

Immediately after the disintegration of the Ottoman empire in World War I, emissaries of President Woodrow Wilson were told by many Arabs in the Middle East that, above all, they sought self-determination. Short of that, they would settle for an American mandate while they fiercely hoped to avoid a French mandate. The picture was clear: France was a symbol of European imperialism, while America stood as the champion of freedom and self-determination and as a decidedly anti-imperial power.

Today, the perceptions have been completely reversed. While the image of France has significantly improved, America's image has collapsed. In a survey I conducted in six Arab countries in May and June of 2004, French President Jacques Chirac was identified as "the most admired world leader" in three of these countries.[1] This despite the fact that many in the Middle East resented his decision to support prohibiting the veil in French public schools. In contrast, President Bush was cited as the second most disliked leader after Prime Minister Ariel Sharon of Israel.

These perceptions are symptomatic of a transformation that has occurred over several decades. Certainly much of this transformation had

---

1. "Arab Attitudes Towards Political and Social Issues, Foreign Policy and Media," public opinion poll conducted jointly by the Anwar Sadat Chair for Peace and Development at the University of Maryland and Zogby International, May–June, 2004.

to do specifically with American policies, especially toward the Arab-Israeli conflict. It began on large scale after the 1967 Arab-Israeli war, which resulted in a humiliating defeat for the Arab side and was followed by clear taking of sides: the U.S. support for Israel and Soviet support for Egypt and Syria. The United States began inheriting on behalf of the West the role that Britain and France had played in prior decades.

There is little doubt that exacerbating the perception of the United States in the Arab world was the role that America began to play as the sole remaining superpower after the collapse of the Soviet Union. Even before the tragedy of 9/11 and the focus on Iraq, there was much resentment of the United States in the Middle East. It is clear that, while this resentment has many causes, the Arab-Israeli issue has been a central factor. It is a "prism of pain" through which most Arabs see the United States. It is the symbol of a collective sense of humiliation and injustice.

Certainly, the Arab-Israeli issue is not the cause of the profound social, political, and economic problems in the Arab world; even if there were peace in the region, the challenges would remain great. But it is the primary prism through which Arabs judge the United States. When they hear an American politician or news of American actions and policies, the first mental act is to focus on those actions and policies that relate to the Arab-Israeli conflict—and those define their ultimate judgment. It is similar, though on a grander scale, to the way 9/11 has become the new prism of pain through which most Americans look at the Middle East. A leader can be wonderful on social, economic, and political issues, but if they sound even remotely sympathetic to al Qaeda terrorism, they will be resented by Americans.

In public opinion surveys that I have conducted over the past few years, majorities of Arabs consistently said that their views of the United States are shaped by policies, not values. Specifically, most Arabs ranked the Arab-Israeli issue as the single most important issue in their priorities. These attitudes have been compounded by the Iraq war and by the war on terrorism that most people in Muslim countries see as a war intended to weaken Muslims. Even the opposition to the Iraq war was in part about the Arab-Israeli issue: Most Arabs saw it as diversion from the Palestinian-Israeli arena that they hoped would be the focal point of American diplomacy after 9/11. Most believed, according to my surveys with Zogby International, that peace in the Middle East will become less likely after the Iraq war.

I say all this not only to point out that actual American policies determine the attitudes toward the United States far more than public diplomacy as such, but also to map out the critical issues for a successful public diplomacy. Many of the surveys that were conducted after 9/11 around the world showed that much of the resentment of American policy is based on a global sense that the United States does not care about others. Ignoring the most painful issues to the public raises questions about policy intentions. It makes it hard for an American leader to argue that we went to war because we care about the welfare of the Iraqi people, when the most painful issue in the region remains ignored. Any successful approach, including in public diplomacy, must at its core be able to project a degree of empathy with regional pain. Recent public opinion trends are very telling in this regard.

A telling measure is the remarkable collapse in the Arab public's trust in the United States in just four years. Certainly, most Arabs have generally viewed American foreign policy as being biased toward Israel. This is not new to the Bush Administration. Every Administration, including those that are seen in historical perspective to have been more balanced, such as the Carter Administration and the Bush-Quayle Administration, was viewed by most Arabs at the time to be biased toward Israel. But this notion of "bias" does not tell the full story. Most Arabs have come to reconcile themselves with the notion that the American-Israeli relationship is special, and that the United States would not sacrifice that relationship to win Arab friendship. What most wanted to believe is that the United States would also take into account Arab grievances and would seek to build on the commonalities of interest in seeking a fair Arab-Israeli peace.

In fact, even though the Clinton Administration at the time was described in the Arab world as being the most pro-Israel administration ever, a survey conducted by the State Department in Saudi Arabia in the spring of 2000 showed that over 60 percent of Saudis expressed confidence in the United States. The reason was obvious: Whatever the public thought of American mediation, the United States was making a significant effort to resolve the conflict and was gearing up for the Camp David Summit. By the fall of 2000, after the collapse of the Camp David negotiations and the inception of the Palestinian Intifada, the confidence had dropped by a third. By the spring, it had dropped further as the intensity of the conflict continued and the new Bush Administration was not focused on this issue.

Since the Afghan and the Iraq wars, the numbers continued to drop rapidly. In my survey in May-June 2004, the percentage of respondents in the region who viewed the United States favorably was in the single digits overall, and less than 4 percent in Saudi Arabia. Confidence in what the United States said had collapsed. Asked whether they believed that the U.S.-led war in Iraq was motivated by the goal of spreading democracy in the region or increasing its prospect for peace, the vast majority in the region disagreed. Most believed that protecting oil and Israel and weakening the Muslim world were the primary American objectives. This collapse of trust in American intentions and in the credibility of the United States is a significant obstacle to an effective American foreign policy.

This issue must be put in historical perspective. Even before the collapse of the budget for global public diplomacy following the end of the Cold War[2] the cards were stacked against effective public diplomacy in the Arab world. While during the Cold War considerable American resources went into effort to build relations with western Europe and also to reach audiences in the former Soviet Union and eastern Europe, little effort was made to communicate directly with Arabs and Muslims. To be sure, there have always been traditional and often fruitful programs administered by the United States Information Agency that have had some impact. But two things limited the effectiveness of these programs: their limited scale compared with the significant expenditure in other regions, and the notion that the United States can happily rely on relations with authoritarian governments in its policy in the region. This last point is important to understanding the United States approach to public diplomacy.

For decades, American foreign policy toward the Middle East focused on relations with authoritarian governments, especially during the Cold War years. In general, the approach was based on the assumption that the United States wields great instruments of influence (both incentives and threats) over governments in the region to assure their compliance or to deter them. Since they are all authoritarian, they were left to their own devices to bring their publics along. Even many of the foreign aid programs, such as those to Egypt, were seen in the end as intended to help the government maintain influence and power at home so that it can stay the course in its cooperative foreign policy with the United States. In that sense, even in programs that were funded by the United States, the Washington approach was not so much to have Washington take credit for them, as to help the governments as a reward for their policy towards the United States.

This approach generally worked, in part because governments had greater capacities to sway their public's opinions. Although there have always been transnational instruments of information, especially radio, most people shaped their opinions on the basis of information obtained from within their own national boundaries, which were mostly monopolized by governments. The information revolution of the 1990s, especially the advent of the transnational Arab satellite television phenomenon, has

---

2. Consider this: In 1980, USAID gave out 20,000 scholarships, compared with 900 in 2003.

changed the game dramatically. Today, most Arabs get their news from sources outside their nation's boundaries. This limits considerably the control of Arab governments over the opinions of their publics.

A good case in point is the concern of Arab governments, such as those in Egypt and Jordan, on the eve of the 2003 war in Iraq. Large majorities of their publics opposed the Iraq war and opposed their governments' cooperation with the United States over that war. But both governments made strategic calculations that led them to cooperate with Washington in any case. This left them with considerable worry that the anti-Americanism in the region that is linked to the war could ultimately hurt their own hold on power. They began an effort to change the mood, especially, in the case of Egypt, through well-covered government statements, and by giving U.S. views more airing. But these efforts had no measurable impact on public opinion, which became even more resentful of the United States. That left insecure governments with one course they knew well: to prevent passionate public opinion from becoming a political problem, they tightened their domestic control even more than before—at the very same time that one stated objective of the Iraq war was to spread democracy. It is no surprise that in my 2004 survey, majorities of Arabs said that the Middle East was even less democratic than it had been before the war.

The challenge for American foreign policy in the coming years is to have an effective approach to the Middle East that does not disregard public opinion or leave it simply to each government to deal with separately. Governments remain the key players in the region, and effective policies cannot disregard them. But public opinion is increasingly relevant and independent from governments. Public diplomacy is an essential arm of effective foreign policy. This proposition must be sorted out.

First, public diplomacy cannot be seen as an alternative to good policy, but as an important supplement which in turn helps to inform policymaking. A puzzling notion has taken hold in the American discourse about foreign policy: policies should not be changed, regardless of public attitudes around the world. There is even a sense that such change may be a sign of weakness. This is an odd position. Interests do not easily change and must be protected even as public attitudes change, but policies are mere instruments to serve interests. If policies fail to serve these interests, they must be changed, for it is interests that are the ends, not policies as such. Public diplomacy, both communicating the American views, and listening to others about theirs, should be an essential component in conveying the effectiveness of policies.

Second, to the extent that one objective in public diplomacy is to build basic trust in the word and stated intentions of the United States, communications must be clear and must take the intended audiences seriously. There are often serious policy differences between the United States and parties in the Middle East, and these cannot be covered up through a public relations campaign. Addressing these differences requires a basic trust in the message, even where there is disagreement. It is important to maintain credible clarity in public diplomacy.

Third, not all issues that are important to the prevalent perceptions of the United States in the Middle East have to do with policies. While the primary anger with the United States relates to real issues and real policies, this anger also helps distort the broader picture of the United States. For example, most Arabs and Muslims have thought that religion and family are not important in American life, even though most Americans think they are central. There is much room for more accurate communication in this area, and this can be done even if there are policy differences. Historically, Arabs and many others around the world differentiated their attitudes toward the United States and the American people from the policies of the U.S. government. While these differences were often exaggerated, it was nonetheless a healthy attitude because it did not translate into a deeper anti-Americanism and because it was more hopeful about the possibilities of change. An increasing concern is that there may be an emerging trend toward a deeper hostility toward America itself. This trend must be reversed.

> A PUZZLING NOTION HAS TAKEN HOLD IN THE AMERICAN DISCOURSE ABOUT FOREIGN POLICY: POLICIES SHOULD NOT BE CHANGED, REGARDLESS OF PUBLIC ATTITUDES AROUND THE WORLD. THERE IS EVEN A SENSE THAT SUCH CHANGE MAY BE A SIGN OF WEAKNESS. THIS IS AN ODD POSITION.

Fourth, effective public diplomacy must be based on the understanding that the target societies in the Middle East are facing their own internal struggles. The key for success is embracing the moderate forces without being the kiss of death. Here, the strategy must be long term and based on building robust relations across important segments of society, including the press, the academy, business, and religious leadership. It requires a sustained effort and far more resources than are now allocated to exchange programs and other efforts in Arab and Muslim countries.

In the end, public diplomacy must be there at the inception of policy: how can you frame an effective policy if you don't take into account how your audience is likely to respond? How could you be sure that the dispensable instruments, the policies themselves, will in the end serve the vital interests of the nation? As more and more Arabs and Muslims express the fear that U.S. policy in the war on terrorism is really a policy intended to weaken the Muslim world, the stakes are higher than ever.

2. "The Last Three Feet": Making the Personal Connection

Kenton W. Keith

The public affairs officer (PAO) position was created to give field direction to the United States Information Agency (USIA) mission, which was, as defined by President Eisenhower in 1953, "to submit evidence to peoples of other nations that the objectives and policies of the United States are in harmony with and will advance their legitimate aspirations." In support of that mission, USIA was to "delineate aspects of American life which facilitate understanding of U.S. government policies." The director of USIA, a sub-cabinet post, had the additional responsibility of advising the president and other senior officials of the psychological consequences abroad of foreign policy options.[1]

These broad mandates shaped both the evolution of USIA's role in the Washington foreign affairs community and the PAO's role within an embassy. Eisenhower's vision carried two separate but complementary roles for USIA: gaining support for U.S. policies and generating understanding of "American life." (The advisory mandate I will discuss below.) In Washington, this gave rise to controversy that deeply influenced the Agency's early years. The argument turned on the question of whether a "policy" (propaganda) agency could gain international credibility as a "cultural" agency. The result was that USIA's policy-driven information role was established as distinct from the more benign people-to-people cultural role, which was set up within the Department of State. However, the PAO in the field was responsible for both tasks. This officer reported directly to the ambassador (and thus indirectly to the Department), but was assigned, supported, and evaluated by USIA. Thus, in spite of the division in responsibility in Washington, it was the PAO who managed all aspects

---

1. USIA was created in August 1953 as part of Reorganization Plan No. 8, as authorized by the Smith-Mundt Act of 1948. The Eisenhower directive defining the Agency's mission was issued on October 22, 1953.

of public diplomacy in the field. It was the PAO who worked to bridge that "last three feet."[2]

In fact, though it has always been a useful image, it is only a partial one. It highlights the reality that the most effective public diplomacy tool has always been one that engaged Americans personally with citizens of a particular country. This would of course include the PAO's personal intervention with a newspaper editor or some other key opinion leader, but it also included the array of programs that put him or her (or members of the public diplomacy staff) into direct, purposeful contact with the wider audience that mattered to American interests. Figuratively, the last three feet were often bridged by U.S. speakers or specialists, by English teachers, by librarians, by Fulbright professors, and of course by other members of the mission, especially a savvy, public affairs-oriented ambassador. That connection was often established in U.S. Information Service (USIS) libraries or cultural centers. I was once chided by a French prime minister who regarded the closure of a popular U.S. cultural center in Paris as mindless.

The personal qualities of our public diplomacy professionals, both American officers and the third-country nationals who have always been an indispensable part of the PAO's staff, were of course critically important. Therefore this group is worth considering briefly in historical perspective.

Not surprisingly, the dual track of PAO responsibility—information and culture—attracted two kinds of practitioner, neither of which resembled very closely their traditional State Department diplomatic colleagues. Until the mid-1960s, USIA officers were not career diplomats. They belonged to a personnel category known as foreign service reserve officers. In the early years, they did not take the foreign service examination, but were recruited for professional experience matched to certain requirements. The cultural officer corps drew on academics, writers, librarians, artists, musicians, athletes. Information specialists had been journalists, veterans of the old Office of War Information, broadcasters, documentary film makers. One final observation about public diplomacy officers in the old USIA: The Agency was able to recruit, train, and assign public diplomacy officers. Officers were recruited for certain skills and promoted for accomplishments that were quite different from those of their State Department colleagues. I have sat on USIA promotion panels evaluating officers from the junior-most ranks to those of the highest level. State officers who served on those

---

2. Edward R. Murrow, Director of USIA under President John F. Kennedy, regularly cited the importance of face-to-face contact in public diplomacy. He said, "The crucial link in the communication chain is the last three feet—one person talking to another."

panels had to learn that those talents their USIA colleagues most valued (program management, language skills, creativity) were significantly different from those that moved State officers most quickly to the top (political or economic analysis, report writing, policy formulation).

The PAO's Advisory Role

According to the original USIA mandate, the director of the Agency had the responsibility of advising the president and senior officials on the probable psychological reaction of foreign audiences to U.S. policy options. As the officer most directly responsible for the shaping of foreign opinion of the United States, it was assumed that his input would be weighed in policy councils. In fact, with rare and notable exceptions, the advisory role of USIA Washington has always been a minor one in foreign policy councils. The director's sub-cabinet rank has been a factor, but need not have been decisive. The personalities and expertise of the succession of directors have also played a role. But even with the high public profile of Edward R. Murrow during the Kennedy years, and despite the personal relationship between Charles Wick and President Reagan, USIA's input on the psychological impact of U.S. actions has been minimal.[3] This was not due to a lack of Agency knowledge; PAOs consistently fed their Washington colleagues pertinent views from the field as part of their justification for various kinds of Agency support.

In the field, however, the PAO has regularly played this role in the tactical implementation of policy. The PAO and the USIS staff, because of their close engagement with a host country's media and intelligentsia, have always been in a position to predict local attitudes. USIS was often—but not always—able to advise Washington on local attitudes via reports from the embassy, which contained contributions from other embassy officers. However, the thrust of these ambassadorial reports was most often an analysis of likely government actions or economic impact, not public attitudes. As deputy director of USIA's Near East area, I frequently sat in on the weekly NEA Affairs Assistant Secretary meetings at State during the final days of the Shah's regime. The weekly review of the embassy's interpretation of events, particularly with regard to growing disaffection in key areas of the public, was at sharp variance with what our USIS staff was telling us.

Incidentally, one putative advantage that was to come from the merger of USIA and State was that public diplomacy would be drawn closer to the

---

3. One notable exception came during the run-up to Desert Shield/Desert Storm in 1990-91, when USIA Arab world experts had a role in briefing the president.

foreign policy formulation process. In the years since the merger, that goal has not been reached. There have been three confirmed undersecretaries of state for public diplomacy since the merger, all of whom have brought records of achievement and recognized skills to the post, but none of whom has had much input into the policymaking process. The first undersecretary was burdened with the sheer magnitude of the human resource and bureaucratic challenge of the merger itself. The second began with a high-energy but ultimately unworkable approach to the use of Madison Avenue techniques in propagating a positive overall image of the United States, and was swept up in post-9/11 challenges, including the war in Afghanistan. The third arrived on the eve of war with Iraq, and stayed in office less than a year. All three have been hampered in their management of the nation's public diplomacy by the flawed structure that resulted from the merger.

Reporting to the undersecretary are the assistant secretary for Educational and Cultural Affairs (who controls resources for exchanges) and the director of International Information Programs (who controls the official Web site, recruits speakers, produces magazines and other media products). However, the undersecretary has no direct connection with the public diplomacy sections in our embassies and no formal connection with the regional bureaus that supervise those posts. The structural flaw has already manifested itself in diminished focus, uncoordinated activities, and reduced field resources.[4]

In short, the undersecretary oversees the U.S. side of the exchanges function and the production of media programs and products, but plays a substantive role neither in the policy formulation process nor in moving the message "the last three feet."

The PAO's Resource Base

The main resource for the PAO has always been people equipped with the tools of communication, persuasion, and cultural influence. The mix of products and programs used to advance U.S. policy in a particular country was the province of the PAO. PAOs were pressed by USIA Washington to improve the quality of identification and interaction with audiences, and to increase reporting on attitudes and "evidence of effectiveness," but they were generally free of the micro-management from deputy chiefs of

---

4. A negotiated blueprint for the merger was completed by teams from the Department of State, USIA, USAID, and the Arms Control and Disarmament Agency in August 1997. It was sent to the secretary of state indicating with bracketed language that no agreement had been reached on how much control the undersecretary should have on field resources and personnel. In any case, the negotiated agreement was never formally adopted and the merger proceeded under State Department direction.

mission and State Department geographic bureaus that has followed the merger.

It has always been essential that a public affairs effort be in synchronization with the policy priorities of the mission. This was achieved first by creating a USIS Country Plan with input from other embassy officers and the approval of the chief of mission; and second by the PAO's regular interaction with the ambassador and the country team. Of critical importance was the approval of the PAO's country plan by the USIA area office. It was this connection to USIA that generated the products and program support the PAO needed to accomplish the mission. It was also a benchmark by which USIA was able to evaluate the PAO's performance.

Elsewhere in this report there are more in-depth examinations of public diplomacy tools, but for those readers unfamiliar with the old USIA products I will briefly note that standing behind the PAO was a remarkable collection of talented, prize-winning, and dedicated men and women who produced the indispensable wireless file, magazines in many languages, pamphlets, radio and television programming for host country media, exhibits, documentary films, and other superb materials. I watched with regret the gradual erosion of this remarkable professional corps, arguably the best the world has ever seen, victims to budget cuts and new technologies.

Still, I believe the most effective programs in the Arab world have remained those that engaged Americans personally with our audiences. These include the daily work of public diplomacy officers who served as information officers or cultural officers, having invested up to two years of their lives in the difficult pursuit of Arabic language skill. I would also include the array of academic and professional exchanges that bring foreign visitors to the United States and American scholars and professors to foreign countries. An important component of this interaction has been the people who run our disappearing cultural centers and libraries, speakers and cultural specialists, and performing artists.

It is hard to overestimate the importance of personal relations in the Arab world. When we returned to Damascus in 1974 after a seven-year hiatus in diplomatic relations, we were welcomed with unexpected warmth. We heard from shopkeepers and government officials alike that their previous guests, Russians and East Germans mainly, were cold and standoffish... not like Americans. It is difficult to judge how much political difference that made, but there were some clues. In less than two years, we were able to establish strong personal relationships with Ministry of Culture officials, a fact I believe helped us to negotiate a cultural agreement that made our activities much less difficult and opened the way for a large educational exchange program.   The Russians had been unsuccessfully seeking such an agreement for years.

Post Management

As an agency head under the old USIA, the PAO had full control of post budget, personnel, equipment, and supplies. The PAO also had authority over his or her vehicles.   While this may seem like an inconsequential issue, having dedicated vehicles was a major advantage for PAOs as they conducted their business, such as delivering routine media documentation to newspapers and TV stations. Moreover, USIS drivers were often trained to use media equipment for off-premises programming.

A key member of the staff in larger posts was the executive officer. In smaller posts, that function was handled by an experienced local employee. That officer made certain that programs operated within budget limits. In addition, as a knowledgeable member of the public diplomacy team, he or she also played the key role of advising the PAO of program options or trade-offs that helped keep priorities covered. A good "exec" had direct links with the budget officer in the USIA area office, who could make adjustments from a central pool to meet urgent program requirements. These were funds that did not compete with other mission needs such as security upgrades or new furniture for the consular waiting room.

The merger of USIA into the State Department meant the PAO was no longer an agency head. Executive officers were often integrated into the embassy management section, and vehicles went into an embassy car pool, as did USIS drivers. While the loss of vehicles hindered but did not cripple PAO efforts, the loss of executive officers put a suffocating paperwork burden on PAOs, many of whom complain that they now have insufficient time to play their essential role outside the embassy: engaging with key audiences.   .

Program Management

It has always been the PAO's job to choreograph an integrated effort that presented and made clear U.S. policies; that promoted a deep and sympathetic understanding of U.S. society, its values, and the achievements of its people; and that actively supported the same basic principles of economic and political freedoms in the host country that exist in the United States. Over the years, it has seemed to me that those goals fell into a natural pattern of activity with short-, medium-, and long-range components.

Short-Range Activities

It is 4 A.M. in Cairo and the phone rings. A plane with passengers of various nationalities (including U.S. citizens) has been hijacked somewhere between

Kabul and Islamabad and is headed in the general direction of Egypt. Or it is mid-morning in Amman and a U.S. official has just been attacked in an assassination attempt. Or the city is Tel Aviv and the U.S. ambassador has been seriously misquoted in an influential newspaper. Of course the incident need not be so dramatic. It rarely is. But these brushfires are a daily fact of life for the PAO in the Arab world. Such incidents may be related to broad, long-standing issues, but there is an immediate public affairs challenge. Local and international media will soon be seeking a statement from the embassy. The government's official spokesman won't be long in trying to find out what the embassy will be saying. And very soon the country team will be meeting in emergency session to assemble information, analyze the incident, and decide what—if anything—the embassy should be saying.

When putting out brushfires, the PAO (or the Information Officer in larger posts) relies on the quality of information at his or her disposal, as well as on an intimate knowledge of relevant policy. At these times, the PAO becomes the voice of the mission and, on some occasions, the voice of the entire U.S. government. That voice must be clear, authoritative, and forthright. It is here that the personal qualities of the PAO as spokesman are most clearly evident.

Medium-Range Activities

The Arab-Israeli dispute, energy security, terrorism, international trade and economic issues, environmental protection, food security: these are just a handful of the thorny issues on the list of the public diplomacy challenges facing the PAO in the Arab and Islamic worlds. Looking at the half-century history of the Middle East dispute, my characterizing it as a "medium-range" problem may seem questionable. By medium range I mean issues or disputes, however intractable or enduring, that have a possible solution from the U.S. perspective. It is the job of the PAO to use the range of tools at his or her disposal to clarify, gain understanding of, and, if possible, gain support for the U.S. view.

Even in this age of instant communication technology, the traditional tools at the PAO's disposal remain valid. Nothing will substitute for the authoritative words of Administration figures. Those words, whether delivered by the Washington File (once known as the Wireless File), text messages, or other means, will always remain indispensable. Even if a mere 15-second sound bite from one of these documents eventually appears on an evening newscast on an Arabic-language satellite channel, the full text will be in the hands of producers, news writers, and print media editors. That may or may not be enough to shape the tone of forthcoming articles, but it will always retain its importance for the record.

An effective tool for PAOs in dealing with these critical ongoing issues is the International Visitor Program, which provides three to four-week professional visits to the United States. Nowadays, visa procedures may mean that getting a visitor cleared takes months instead of weeks, but the program retains its value. This interpersonal program is another way to cross that critical "three feet." So, too, is the well-chosen speaker, who can be slotted into a think-tank round-table discussion, a university seminar, or simply a luncheon with the right opinion leader.

In practice, it is the mix of resources applied to an issue over a sustained period that is often the best chance of achieving positive outcomes. In Qatar we launched a campaign to improve the protection of U.S. copyrighted material. Armed with messages of concern from relevant U.S. government agencies, the ambassador and the PAO made personal *demarches* to senior ministerial contacts. The Qataris acknowledged that they were already considering legislation to halt the open commerce of pirated computer software and other materials, but were concerned about citizen reaction. The PAO enlisted the help of Qatari musicians (whose own material was routinely pirated) for a series of interviews in the local press. Then she organized a well-targeted International Visitor program for the officials charged with writing the legislation. They returned from their trip convinced of the need for this protection and had already arranged for U.S. technical assistance in the drafting of legislation. The result was a law protecting copyrighted material that was clear and enforceable.

Long-Range Activities: Shifting Ground

Perceptions of the United States as a society—its values, aims, institutions, and attitudes—have not usually been at the top of most Arab world PAOs' list of concerns. Too often these long-range concerns have been pushed to the side by more burning issues. The cultural affairs officer (or the equivalent foreign service national in the smallest posts) was assumed to be managing the Fulbright program and the cultural center (where they existed), knitting enduring relationships with universities and other cultural institutions, and perhaps bringing the occasional pianist to perform in the ambassador's salon. Meanwhile, the important work of supporting current policies through information work claimed most of the PAO's time. At the same time that budget cuts have claimed much of the cultural affairs infrastructure—U.S. and foreign service national positions, cultural centers, libraries—a dramatic estrangement has taken hold. Andy Kohut, executive director of the Pew Research Center for the People and the Press, frequently cites alarming statistics indicating that anti-U.S. attitudes abroad have moved from "anger" to "loathing."[5] It is frequently heard that overseas audiences hate us for what we stand for and envy us for what we have. Frankly, my experience in the Arab world over a period of three decades does not bear this out.

Immediately after 9/11 Americans were asking, "Why do they hate us?" My own question over the years was, "Why, when their central, unanimously held belief was that the United States almost single-handedly sustained the greatest tragedy in their modern history—the existence and well-being of Israel—did they like us so much? Why, when most Arabs believed the United States was instrumental in the humiliating defeats of 1967 and 1973, did they continue to look to the United States for higher education, economic opportunity, and cultural inspiration? How could it be that even in times of deeply strained relations between their countries—indeed, when there were no relations at all—Arabs would tell us they liked Americans, they just didn't like our government? What was it they saw in the American experience that appealed to them in spite of everything? These were important questions if your business was dealing with attitudes.

The challenge for American public diplomacy in the early years of USIA was to convince the Arab world that we sought a just and permanent solution to the Arab-Israeli dispute while reinforcing the generally positive feeling Arabs had toward the United States. The most effective tools were our cultural centers and libraries, our educational exchange programs, and cultural and sports presentations. USIA's Arab language book translation program put into the hands of Arab readers the basic texts of American government, biographies of our most important political figures, and the classics of American literature. Agency magazines like *al Majal* were widely distributed. They portrayed a dynamic, successful society in which Americans with Arab origins were full participants. Even with its institutional racism and economic inequalities, and despite its unpopular war in Vietnam, America represented an ideal of opportunity and personal liberty.

A significant change arrived with the success of the Islamic Revolution in Iran in 1979: Khomeini's vision of an Islamic world whose organizing principles included open conflict with the United States on both religious and political grounds. For the first time, Islamic activists in the Arab world had the example of a society that could be run on Islamic principles and remain independent from both East and West.

---

5. See Andrew Kohut, "Anti-Americanism: Causes and Characteristics" (Washington, DC: Pew Research Center for the People and the Press, December 10, 2003). See also the Pew Global Attitudes Project reports, especially *What the World Thinks in 2002* (Washington, DC: Pew Research Center for the People and the Press, 2002) and *Views of a Changing World* (Washington, DC: Pew Research Center for the People and the Press, 2003).

A Re-Energized American Public Diplomacy for the Region

For the first time, our public diplomacy effort is shaped by a concern that anti-American *Islamic* sentiment, combined with Arab opposition to U.S. support to Israel, could have expanding appeal in the Arab world and a lasting impact on our position in the region. By the late 1980s, our closest friends in the Arab world were facing serious internal challenges from political Islam. It is difficult to deny that, by any objective measurement, these governments are not meeting the needs of their citizens. Indeed almost no Arab government is. Education systems are failing, social services are weak, job opportunity is dismal. Desert Storm freed Kuwait, but the U.S. military presence that remained in the region became the focus for ongoing anti-American actions in the Arabian peninsula and beyond, including the tragedy of 9/11.

Jihadists in the Arab and Islamic worlds point to our military action in Afghanistan and Iraq as evidence that their religion is under siege. When I served as spokesman for the coalition during the war in Afghanistan, the Muslim media corps remained suspicious of the coalition's aims. Our press briefings were faithfully covered daily, but the reporting slant was hostile and accusatory. We made a special effort to interact with the Arab media, giving backgrounders, informal talks over tea, on-camera interviews, and so on. But the belief persisted that the coalition was acting with overwhelming and indiscriminate force against the Muslim population of Afghanistan *because they were Muslims who had defied the will of the United States.*

The perception in the Arab world is that Americans are rigorously anti-Islam, and that after 9/11 the U.S. government has reflected this sentiment in a variety of ways. U.S. visa policies since 9/11 have drastically reduced the number of Muslim students and medical travelers who come to the United States. The U.S. government's official pronouncements speak of safe borders and open doors; yet, for most young Arabs and Muslims, the door to U.S. study or travel does not seem open. Refusal rates are high among young men. Many potential travelers have been discouraged by stories of delays and harassment at the borders. American education, a $13 billion industry prior to 9/11, is losing market share to Europe, Australia, New Zealand, and Canada. Some countries whose official language is not English have instituted new degree programs conducted in English to handle Arab and Muslim students who want to study in English but choose to avoid the stigmatization they face in the United States. In reality, the loss of market share in international education is far less important than the loss of this potential corps of people who would have come to know and understand us in the most effective way. This is a problem we must deal with head on.

As long as U.S. policy toward the Palestinian-Israeli dispute remains as deeply unpopular across the region as it is at present, it would be naïve to think that rapid positive change in attitudes toward the United States is possible. It isn't. However, gradual change, using the long-range tools at our disposal, may be. U.S. engagement with policy in the region is vital to the success of long-term outcomes. Following the Madrid peace talks, the United States was deeply engaged in moving the process forward, and in a short time rather remarkable change took place. When Syrians and Israelis shook hands across a table in a Madrid school building, it was a significant step. It would not have happened without an active, aggressive U.S. role.

> LET US IMAGINE AN INITIATIVE IN WHICH THE PRESIDENT SAYS, "I AM SENDING YOU MORE OF OUR YOUTH TO GET TO KNOW YOU BETTER, AND I AM ASKING YOU TO SEND US MORE OF YOURS."

In addition, exchange programs, cultural centers, and direct contact between public diplomacy officers and audiences in the field—all proven tools—could make a difference if they were funded adequately. The amount spent on public diplomacy programs at present is about three-tenths of one percent of the military budget.

Meanwhile, another old-fashioned public diplomacy action could have far-reaching impact. I would like to see our leaders speak directly to the Islamic world about our vision of its future relationship with the United States. That vision may not be one completely shared by the Islamic world, but it could offer reassurance that they really matter to us. Let us imagine an initiative in which the president says, "I am sending you more of our youth to get to know you better, and I am asking you to send us more of yours." Or perhaps the president might sign into law an act establishing government funding for the study of Arabic, Farsi, Pashtu and other regional languages. Gestures matter in the Arab and Muslim worlds.

Finally, the effort to reach younger audiences with our exchange programs deserves encouragement—and more funding. High school exchange programs are comparatively inexpensive, yet priceless.

This is slow, incremental work. It is hard to sustain in an atmosphere that demands rapid results. Enlightened leadership, such as that of Dwight Eisenhower's, will be needed if we are to truly persuade the Arab and Islamic worlds that our objectives and policies "are in harmony with and will advance their legitimate aspirations."

3. The Uses of Modern Technology in Public Diplomacy

Barry Fulton

The U.S. government should…communicate and defend American ideals in the Islamic world, through much stronger public diplomacy to reach more people, including students and leaders outside of government. Our efforts here should be as strong as they were in combating closed societies during the Cold War.

—National Commission on Terrorist Attacks upon the United States.[1]

Public diplomacy—a small but critical part of the nation's foreign policy assets—requires reform. As I hope to demonstrate, technology itself is not the answer, but it can enable a strategy for the conduct of public diplomacy.

Canadian scholar Harold Innis has shown that new technologies have profoundly influenced social order throughout history by creating what he calls "cultural disturbances." New technologies—faster and less expensive —crowd out not only existing technologies, but also the social order that supports them. It is not a historical anomaly that Microsoft declared an unprecedented dividend to stockholders earlier this year, while AT&T stumbles toward bankruptcy. New technologies eclipse the old.

Ten years ago, the *Washington Times* criticized USIA for its innovative approach to disseminating information via the Internet and other digital technologies. Fearing that traditional modes of communication had been abandoned, the editorial sarcastically asked "how many computer whizzes there are in China or Burma or Cuba or Tibet, or Russia for that matter."[2]

---

1. National Commission on Terrorist Attacks upon the United States, *The 9/11 Commission Report* (Washington, DC: GPO, 2004), Executive Summary, 18.
2. "The Death of an Agency," *Washington Times*, August 11, 1994.

The advances poor countries have made in adopting new technologies notwithstanding,[3] some will ask the same question today: Does technology have a public diplomacy role in the Arab and Islamic worlds? I will argue in this essay that we poorly serve U.S. national interest if we do not strategically exploit information technology in engaging Islamic publics. Indeed, one constant in public diplomacy has been its early adoption of new technologies, whether it was radio, motion pictures, high-speed printing, television, or the Internet.

Gutenberg's invention of movable type challenged the authority of the Catholic Church and led indirectly to the Reformation. The spirit of the enlightenment led to a free press, which in turn hastened the rise of democratic governments. Similarly, the evidence is compelling that the media that penetrated the Iron Curtain during the Cold War, particularly government-sponsored short-wave radio, kept alive the promise of freedom in eastern Europe and the Soviet Union. As borders become more porous, ideas become more threatening to the survival despotic regimes. Arab governments have recognized that al Jazeera is not just an annoyance, but a threat to their stability.

Technology is not necessarily benign. Ayatollah Khomeini used cassette tapes to fuel the Iranian revolution, Osama bin Laden has skillfully used videotapes to communicate to the world, and terrorists sustain their worldwide networks through the Internet.

Although our attention to the Islamic world is driven by 9/11, it would be a mistake to argue that information technology, as a tool of public diplomacy, will serve as a short-term antidote to the anger directed toward the United States and its policies. In his 1961 classic, *The Wretched of the Earth*, Frantz Fanon observed that Algerians drenched in hopelessness evoked violence as a means of communication. "It frees the native from his inferiority complex and from his despair and inaction; it makes him fearless and restores his self-respect."[4]

Four decades later, the conditions about which Fanon wrote continue to influence perceptions of the West. Although only a miniscule few Muslims engage in terrorism, we cannot ignore the widespread and growing support for terrorists in the Islamic world. For example, data from the Pew Research Center for the People and the Press from March 2004 show that Osama bin Laden is viewed favorably by large percentages in Pakistan (65 percent), Jordan (55 percent), and Morocco (45 percent).[5] At the same

---

3. China, for instance, has surpassed all but the United States in Internet connectivity.

4. Frantz Fanon, *The Wretched of the Earth*, trans. Constance Farrington (New York: Grove Press, 1965 [reprint of French edition, Paris, 1961]), 94.

5. *A Year After Iraq War* (Washington, DC: Pew Research Center for the People and the Press, 2004).

time, in a six-country poll conducted by Zogby International in June 2004, support for U.S. policy on terrorism ranged from a high of only 21 percent in Jordan to a low of 2 percent in Saudi Arabia.[6]

In the three years since 9/11, the U.S. image abroad has been in free fall. For a host of reasons, not the least of which is "a decent respect to the opinion of mankind," the United States is obliged to respond. Since 9/11, government reaction to its sinking public image has been tentative and tepid.

> THERE IS NO SERIOUS EVIDENCE THAT SUGGESTS THAT FUNDAMENTAL ATTITUDE CHANGE IS A SIMPLE REACTION TO THE OCCASIONAL MESSAGE THAT PENETRATES THE BABBLE OF DISSENTING VOICES.

Practitioners can cite endless anecdotes and compelling statistics to show the value of exchange programs, libraries, cultural programs, and other public diplomacy activities that bring foreign publics in sustained contact with their American peers. But none of these programs has the critical mass to make a sustained difference. Most of them are in decline, and even those that have been sustained are handicapped by visa delays and bureaucratic caution.

Although we honor the value of exchanges, the attention of senior planners tends to focus far more on the message, implying that if the words are carefully chosen and well packaged, those who now express contempt for America will have a change of heart. There is no serious evidence that suggests that fundamental attitude change is a simple reaction to the occasional message that penetrates the babble of dissenting voices.

If there was any doubt when the public diplomacy campaign was launched in 2002, it is now clear that branding is not the answer, nor are occasional videos and pamphlets that demonstrate common values. In short, there are two fundamental weaknesses with the current approach: (1) the scale of activities, many of which are meritorious, is vastly disproportionate to the problem; and (2) the belief that the message constitutes the core of public diplomacy is misguided.

Technology and Social Networks

There are few successful practitioners of public diplomacy who will not recognize themselves as players in a social network. Those whom we would influence are related to many others in loosely connected and overlapping networks, from which one learns values, hones beliefs, and develops attitudes. These networks are families, tribes, religions, corporations,

---

6. Zogby International, "Impressions of America," poll conducted in June 2004.

universities, and clubs, and their influence vastly exceeds that of the most sophisticated information campaign. While these social networks—held together by tradition, by ritual, and by ideas—are often impervious to outside influences, there are exceptions. As every political campaign appreciates, influencing the undecided and energizing the apathetic are realizable goals.

By mapping social networks to show how each person is connected to others, there emerge critical links through whom information and influence flow. They are leaders who have the respect of many, and to whom many turn for advice. In a world of limited resources, they are the people whom public diplomacy practitioners would target for attention. Finding them, however, is an exercise that requires skill and time—both scarce resources. Even if the critical nodes of the network cannot be located, recognizing and interacting within the network is an essential first step. That, too, it must be stressed, is difficult, particularly in cultures distant from our own.

What do social networks have to do with information technology? The Internet is a powerful enabler, allowing networks to flourish across borders. As David Ronfeldt and colleagues have chronicled in *The Zapatista Social Netwar in Mexico*, the Zapatistas' information operations caused the government to halt combat operations against them and turn to political dialogue and negotiations.[7] There are numerous other examples. The homegrown campaign against landmines reached critical mass in 1997 through the Internet and resulted in an international treaty, while the U.S. government stood on the sidelines. Similarly, anti-globalization activists have used the Internet to organize protest movements that shut down top-level international negotiations.

Social networks are as old as civilization. The difference today is that the amplifying power of technology enables social organizations to extend across borders. Its power lies not in the linear, one-to-many dynamic of the broadcaster or the Webcaster, but in the often loosely organized and spontaneous interaction of many individual activists. Those who would influence others through control rather than empowerment will find no little irony in the robust international connectivity facilitated by the Internet, courtesy of research sponsored by the Department of Defense.

The Noosphere

Arquilla and Ronfeldt, drawing on the writings of the French theologian Pierre Teilhard de Chardin, suggest that the rich, unregulated connectivity

---

7. David Ronfeldt, John Arquilla, Graham E. Fuller, and Melissa Fuller, *The Zapatista Social Netwar in Mexico* (Santa Monica, CA: Rand, 1998).

evolving in our digital world is leading to a higher social consciousness as we increasingly exchange information with other cultures and grow from the experience.[8] Teilhard variously described this social consciousness as a globe-spanning realm of "the mind," a "thinking circuit," a "stupendous thinking machine," a "thinking envelope" full of fibers and networks, and a planetary "consciousness." With terrorism and genocide continually in the news, the promise of an evolving noosphere may be faulted, while such unpredictable changes as the breakup of the Soviet Union and the end of Apartheid in South Africa give reason for optimism. America has been a beacon because it gave hope to many, particularly those trapped in repressive societies. The social networks amplified by information technology provide a vehicle for the return of hope; that is, if we develop a strategic communication plan that is coupled with avenues for social change.

Spheres of Influence

Practitioners of public diplomacy understand that their business is about persuasion, even as they understand how demanding is their art. The most successful are recognized as those who empathize with their interlocutors, understand their brief, and excel in persuasive dialogue. In his insightful book *The Tipping Point*, Malcolm Gladwell lays out a calculus for action that involves three distinct skills.[9] The three skills are represented by what Gladwell calls *connectors*, *mavens*, and *salesmen*. The *connector* is a person who knows everyone in her community, who enjoys expanding her circle of friends, who is turned to by others for advice. She is one of the critical nodes in the social network—or if the culture doesn't allow, is at least a recognized member of the network. The *maven* is a person who cares about knowledge, who would go out of his way to attend a lecture or read a book. He cares far less about connecting. The *salesman* is the person who closes the deal, who plays that one-dimensional role that many mistake for public diplomacy. She is a part of the team, but will fail without the others. In a wired world they all have a role, but without the *connector* to press the flesh, the *maven* and the *salesman* will be left adrift. The ideal public diplomat would embody all three types. As that is seldom, if ever, possible, a strategic communication plan must draw on diverse talents to ensure successful communication.

---

8. John Arquilla and David Ronfeldt, *The Emergence of Noopolitik* (Santa Monica: Rand, 1999).

9. Malcolm Gladwell, *The Tipping Point: How Little Things Can Make a Big Difference* (New York: Little, Brown, 2000).

Putting Our Money where Our Mouth Is

A host of studies have chronicled the problem. The U.S. Advisory Group on Public Diplomacy for the Arab and Muslim World called for a "dramatic transformation in public diplomacy—in the way the U.S. communicates its values and policies to enhance our national security."[10] Its 2003 report, *Changing Minds, Winning Peace*, noted bluntly: "The transformation requires an immediate end to the absurd and dangerous underfunding of public diplomacy in a time of peril…"[11] The Council on Foreign Relations was no less candid in its call for reform: "Hatred and ill will toward the United States and its policies are dangerous and growing, and…radical changes are needed in response."[12] Of the dozen or so reports completed in the past eighteen months, there is no dissent from the view that soft power, to use Joseph Nye's phrase, is a national resource that is undervalued and inadequately leveraged. If there is any doubt, compare 2004 allocations to defense, intelligence, and public diplomacy (including Alhurra TV, Radio Sawa, and Voice of America) (figure 1).

FIGURE 1.   2004 dollars spent on defense, intelligence, and public diplomacy (in billions)

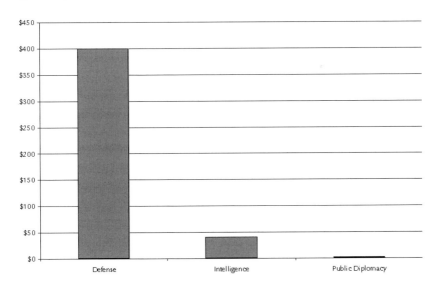

---

10. Edward P. Djerejian, *Changing Minds, Winning Peace: A New Strategic Direction for U.S. Public Diplomacy in the Arab and Muslim World*, report of the U.S. Advisory Group on Public Diplomacy for the Arab and Muslim World (Washington, DC: 2003), 8.

11. Ibid.

12. *Finding America's Voice: A Strategy for Reinvigorating U.S. Public Diplomacy* (New York: Council on Foreign Relations, 2003), vi.

Recognizing the problem, however, does not mean that the solution is evident. And spending more money does not necessarily mean that minds will change and peace will break out in the Middle East. The several reports rightly call for more resources, organizational reform, deployment of modern media, engagement of the private sector—and a great deal more of everything that has worked in the past. There is wisdom in all of that, but not a strategic vision.

A New Vision

There are four obvious and profound problems that the United States must confront in developing a strategic vision for the conduct of public diplomacy in the Arab and Muslim worlds: policy, perceptions, demographics, and knowledge.

Some have faulted the several reports for sidestepping **policy** issues. It is not, some say, that we are misunderstood, but that we are all too well understood. Indeed, policy formulation and articulation must be at the core of any public diplomacy strategy. Public opinion should not drive policy, but must inform policy. It must be understood that if policies drive populations away from America, our strategic interests will suffer.

Perceptions are the realities on which people act. And policies with which people disagree become grossly exaggerated. Unless these perceptions are understood and addressed through a spirited exchange, they will, like the Protocols of Zion, exist as unshakable beliefs.

There are, in addition, two burgeoning obstacles to returning to a fruitful relation with the Arab and Muslim worlds: **demographics** and **knowledge**. Of the planet's one billion Muslims, half are under the age of 25. Half of Pakistan's 159 million are under the age of 20. We must ask what future these 80 million young Pakistanis face. (The American cohort under the age of 20 is virtually the same size, although it constitutes less than 30 percent of the U.S. population).[13] How might their lives change if the United States reorganizes its public diplomacy strategy, doubles exchanges, and adopts modern technology? Many young Muslims are forming their knowledge of the 21st century with a 15th century education. Another information campaign will not make a difference unless it is one piece of a much larger vision. The short answer—and long-term solution—is education.

The authoritative and bold *Arab Human Development Report 2003* paints a disturbing report of education in the Middle East. Warning that

---

13. Population data is drawn from the U.S. Census Bureau, available on the Web at www.census.gov/ipc/www/idbsum.html.

the quality of Arab education is declining, the report asserts that "the present state of Arab higher education prevents it from contributing effectively to the creation of a knowledge society."[14]   UNDP Regional Director Rima Khalaf Hunaidi writes that the goal of this far-reaching study is to "activate a dialogue among Arabs on ways to change the course of Arab history and afford the Arab people the decent lives to which they aspire and to which they are entitled."[15]

India and China provide examples to emulate in the Middle East. The Institute of International Education's annual *Open Doors* report shows Indian student enrollment at American universities last year increased by 12 percent to 75,000, and Chinese student enrollment increased to 65,000.[16] On the other hand, student enrollment from all countries in the Middle East declined by 10 percent to an aggregate of just 35,000, including only 4,000 from Saudi Arabia. It is hardly a coincidence that years of attention to higher education in India and China have been followed by high growth rates, while the Middle East has stagnated.

The U.S. Role in Exploiting Information Technology

As represented in my 2002 study, *Leveraging Technology in the Service of Diplomacy*:

> Diplomacy and information technology intersect at three levels. The first is that which promotes efficiency in existing business practices including payrolling, accounting, and contracting. The second level directly supports the conduct of diplomacy including reporting, negotiation, representation, and advocacy. The third level is the substance rather than the practice of diplomacy. It includes U.S. negotiations to open telecommunications markets in China, analysis of the impact of software production in India, and advancement of telecommunications deregulation in the Caribbean.[17]

---

14. UNDP, *Arab Human Development Report 2003: Building a Knowledge Society* (New York: UNDP, 2003), 168.

15. UNDP, *A Call to "Reclaim Arab Knowledge,"* news release, October 20, 2003. Available at http://www.undp.org/rbas/ahdr/englishpresskit2003.html/.

16. Institute of International Education, *Open Doors 2003: International Students in the United States* (New York: IIE, November 2003). Data available at http://opendoors.iienetwork.org/.

17. Barry Fulton, *Leveraging Technology in the Service of Diplomacy: Innovation in the Department of State* (Arlington, VA: PricewaterhouseCoopers Endowment for The Business of Government, 2002.)

Efficiencies at level one have been continually introduced to support diplomacy.   At level two, the conduct of public diplomacy—despite occasional claims to the contrary—has kept pace with evolving technologies, reflecting a practice over a period of five decades. USIA was among the first U.S. government entities to introduce Web sites, digital video conferencing, and interactive CD-ROMs in the early 1990s. The State Department's international Web site—updated each day in several languages, including Arabic and Persian—is a model of its kind.

The Washington File, which began more than a half century ago, is now available through the Web, by subscription, on personal digital assistants, and in some instances through hand-delivered hard copies. It is targeted to traditional readers as well as to innovators. Virtual Presence posts, which feature a Web site and occasional personal visits, are now operating in Egypt, Bangladesh, Russia, and Brazil—in cities where a physical presence cannot be supported. A *demarche*, a time-honored written communiqué, was recently delivered to European ministries accompanied by a link to a State Department Web site to build support for humanitarian relief in Sudan. More than 100 missions are now posting political and economic reporting on a classified Web site available to other U.S. government departments. Projects initiated and completed under Secretary Powell's leadership include desktop access by all employees to the Internet, a substantially improved classified network, the integration of the public diplomacy network with other State Department networks, and upgraded security for all State Department information applications. Work is underway on a state-of-the-art messaging, archival, and retrieval system that will integrate e-mail, cables, and memoranda through a worldwide electronic network. A laggard in information technology in the nineties, the Department of State has resumed its leadership role in the use of information technology. These advances have been marked by the Office of Management and Budget, which recently granted its highest score to the State Department for progress in managing its information technologies.

The recommendations of the U.S. Advisory Group on Public Diplomacy for the Arab and Muslim World for upgrading information technology are all sound, and could be implemented without a major increase in resources. They build on an innovative base, but do not represent a novel approach for the post-9/11 environment.

Apart from Alhurra TV and Radio Sawa, practically all of the government's public diplomacy programming is aimed at providing information to influentials. Talk of reaching a broader and younger audience is hollow when these new audiences can be counted in the hundreds or thousands. The programs are well conceived and executed, but their scale doesn't match the need. Information was a valuable resource in an earlier age of information scarcity. Today, those to whom our messages are aimed, like the rest of us, are struggling to cope with information overload. And when one applies a mental filter to deal with this flood of new information, trusted sources are first in the queue. That leaves the United States in a virtual dead-letter box. Our effectiveness is undercut to the degree that we emphasize messages and channels over the utility of the information. To borrow a maxim from the intelligence community, we should not focus on information, but on *actionable* information—or better yet, on knowledge.

What Can Be Done by Washington?

It is no accident that a chapter on technology has given relatively little space to technology. Technology is a means, not the end. It is a means to extend our voices, to amplify our actions. If we try to exploit our interlocutors through our superior technology, success will be limited to the short term. If, however, we aim to exploit the technologies to address the key questions of policy, perception, demographics, and knowledge, we can make a difference. If we come to understand that public diplomacy is not about words that are cast to the ignorant, but about ideas that are debated, about knowledge that enables action, about lifting people from despair to hope, *then* we can address the root causes of the issues that separate us.

A comprehensive strategic plan is beyond this paper, although it is self-evident that a critical strategic role for public diplomacy is to address the failure of two major institutions in the Middle East: universities and the press. Both must be done in cooperation with Arab and Islamic nations. Some will reject the proposition that the United States has a role, but for those who welcome the initiative, long-term goals could be established for reforming both universities and the press. Information technology can be used wholesale to provide materials online with copyright wavers, to develop distant learning, to create cooperative joint degree programs, to ease visa restrictions, to signal that the scientific knowledge base of the United States is a worldwide resource that can be tapped by countries whose futures rest in the balance. As Moore's Law predicted, the costs of computers and connectivity continue to decrease each year, with the consequence that the opportunities for cooperative knowledge sharing increase proportionately.

The United States, also in cooperation with interested Arab and Islamic countries, should fund a Middle Eastern Press Consortium involving the finest journalism schools in the United States. Students, scholars, journalists, and editors would then have an opportunity to be exposed to Western ideals of objectivity and fair play, with the conviction that after several generations, the one-sided and distorted image of America that often appears in the Middle Eastern press would be attenuated. The United States should offer this opportunity, not because we expect our press model to prevail, but because our model demonstrates that there is more than one view of reality. The role of the fourth estate has always acted as a counterbalance to the autocratic tendencies of government. It could serve a similar role in the Middle East if we have the patience.

The cost of these two initiatives? Ten, twenty times what we devote to public diplomacy in the region now. As a starting point, why not use the per capita funding devoted to information activities in Germany and Austria after World War II, which, adjusted for inflation, would equal about $1 billion annually for the Arabic and Islamic populations of the world. It is expensive by current public diplomacy standards, but a bargain compared with expenditures for projecting hard power.

What Can be Done in the Field?

Once the staff reaches critical mass through an unprecedented increase in resources, its role will be discovering, joining, expanding, creating, and participating in social networks. This requires *connectors, mavens*, and *salesmen*, as well as the exploitation of information technology, including contact management systems, sophisticated databases for identifying, recording, and sustaining person-to-person contacts. It will require officers who are media professionals, academics, and artists who can join networks of peers. It will require a long-term strategic vision where each officer builds on the work of his or her predecessor. It will require professional discipline, as much of the contact work takes time and patience.

Finally, it will require a redefinition of public diplomacy itself. Public diplomacy must be aided by level one technology for workplace efficiency. It must involve level two technologies to ensure connectivity. But at the third level, it must also enable the nations of the Arab and Islamic world to adopt the technological and intellectual advances that characterize the 21st century. The practitioners in the field must understand that their role is to act as a catalyst for the advance of knowledge, not simply the propagation of information. There is no guarantee that exploiting new technologies will have the positive effect that is envisioned, although the potential of technology to change society is undisputed.

Conclusion

The 9/11 Commission report concluded that long-term success demands the use of all elements of national power—including public diplomacy. The report asks the United States to support Pakistani President Musharraf's call for enlightened moderation. And it notes approvingly that Saudi Crown

Prince Abdullah has embraced the *Arab Human Development Report*. The Commission recognized that hard power must be complemented by the strategic use of soft power in the post-9/11 environment.

The commissioners explicitly call for the United States to engage in the struggle for ideas: "In short, the United States has to help defeat an ideology, not just a group of people, and we must do so under difficult circumstances."[18] There is no element of the federal government better prepared to coordinate this effort than the public diplomacy practitioners of the Department of State—but only if they are given adequate resources and the means to serve as the leading edge of a nationwide consortium of educators, intellectuals, artists, NGOs, and businesses. State Department diplomatists understand that it is in our mutual interest to take this long-range gamble. It is a gamble because there is no guarantee of success. It is a gamble because a short-lived effort without follow-through for generations may well be money wasted. But it is a prudent gamble because, unlike the old Jack Benny joke, we should not pause when we are faced with the choice between our money or our life.

Public diplomacy will not defeat terrorism. But the breeding grounds for terrorism will be far less fertile if a public diplomacy strategy encompasses policy, perceptions, demographics, and education.

Information technology is not the silver bullet, but it does allow engagement of whole populations, and it does accelerate engagement when time is short. To summarize my earlier observations on networking, information technology for the sake of delivering messages alone will not suffice. The model is not broadcasting, Webcasting, or narrowcasting. It is better characterized as the EBay model. This $24 billion online marketplace, with more than 100 million members, is wildly successful. People across the globe can trade efficiently with very low transaction costs. EBay manages the forum for exchange, and leaves it to buyers and sellers to engage. CEO Margaret Whitman has guided EBay into one of the greatest commercial Internet success stories by changing the paradigm of marketing. She says, "I think it takes a little while to understand this dynamic, self-regulating economy. Most business people want to control, and they want to drive. EBay is much more of an enabler. We say here, 'We enable; we don't direct.' And that is the fundamental thing that people have to understand."[19]

To engage publics in the Middle East, public diplomacy practitioners must enable, not direct. This concept, which captures the spirit of the

---

18. National Commission on Terrorist Attacks upon the United States, *The 9/11 Commission Report* (Washington, DC: GPO, 2004), 376.

19. Nick Wingfield, "Auctioneer to the World," *Wall St. Journal*, August 5, 2004.

Fulbright legislation, is driven by ideas, not ideology. It is built on respect for human relations, and abetted by information technology. Instead of the focus on messages and channels that has constrained the post-9/11 conversation, it will serve to enable peoples now trapped by despair and inaction.

4. The Role of the Embassy Public Affairs Officer After 9/11

James L. Bullock

This chapter is one officer's view from the field, an "up close" assessment of our official public engagement with the Arab and Islamic worlds in mid-2004.[1] Specifically, this chapter looks at the daily work of our public diplomats overseas. Rather than address specific programs in detail, I will focus on some of the day-to-day operating challenges that hinder their efforts to influence Arab and Muslim public opinion. I see three main areas for improvement in our public diplomacy regarding Arabs and Muslims: overall resources (especially personnel), technology, and bureaucratic structure. The discussion that follows spells out why I believe we must do better in these areas.

Unfortunately, I do not yet see any general U.S. consensus emerging as to what exactly our public diplomacy priorities should be toward Arabs and Muslims. I hope the comments that follow will make a positive contribution to the current debate and help to advance the effectiveness of our public diplomacy in this important part of the world.

September 11 Was More About Us Than about Them

The attacks on the World Trade Center and the Pentagon in September 2001 significantly changed American perceptions of the Arab and Islamic worlds. Those events did not, however, mark a correspondingly significant change in the Arab and Islamic worlds. The daunting political, economic, and social problems of those regions continued to challenge the best efforts of would-be reformers both from within these regions and beyond. What changed most on 9/11 was our own awareness as Americans of these problems. They had boiled over and burned us.

---

1. The ideas presented in this chapter are the personal views of the author. They do not reflect official U.S. policy or represent official views of the U.S. Department of State.

Fortunately, some of us were already paying attention. Although little-known to the average American back home, a talented corps of Arabic-speaking foreign service officers had long been working from within our embassies and consulates in every Arab and Islamic country to reach out to local populations. After 9/ll, these officers dutifully carried on, organizing exchanges, engaging local media, encouraging the study of English, assisting American scholars, programming visiting speakers, and promoting our ideas and values to elite and general audiences alike.

These specialized public affairs officers (PAOs) have carried on since 9/11, but their work has become more difficult to execute, and their value to our overall national interests has increasingly been questioned. Meanwhile, international hostility to America's Middle East policies has been on the rise. Three years after the terrorist attacks of 9/11, we Americans agonize over the latest reports that Arab and Muslim opinions of the United States—the sole remaining superpower and self-proclaimed defender of democracy—are strongly negative and dropping to all-time lows. In Egypt, for example, the largest Arab country and a key U.S. Middle East ally, fully 98 percent of the population reportedly holds a negative view of the United States.[2] I do not believe, however, that this reflects any basic enmity toward the American people, our values, or our way of life. Quite the contrary: most Arabs and Muslims are still attracted to the values we espouse, but they also almost universally reject what they see as our unconditional defense of their great rival, our unwarranted military occupation of a major Arab country, and our continued accommodation of repressive regimes, from North Africa to Southeast Asia. In the resulting atmosphere of suspicion and mistrust, our PAOs in the Arab and Islamic worlds now face unprecedented challenges addressing audiences even on relatively noncontroversial topics.

If we truly are paying more attention now to what is happening in these regions, we will recognize that understanding personal relationships is key to understanding Arabs and Muslims. Cultural differences matter. Perhaps because America is a nation of immigrants, we grow up looking to the future more than to the past, generally seeking to reinvent ourselves through our own work and study and personal initiative. In the Arab world, for a mix of reasons, social and economic opportunity is less widely available, and individuals cling more tightly to familial, religious, and historical identities. Characteristically, our collective response as Americans to the bad news coming from the Arab and Islamic worlds since 9/11 has not been to look inward, but rather to look forward. We feel we must "do something," such as launch new programs to burnish our image abroad,

2. Zogby International, "Impressions of America," poll conducted in June 2004.

and throw our marketing might at what many perceive to be first and foremost a public relations problem. Some resources have been allocated, but rebuilding our relationship with the Arab and Muslim worlds will take more than just money.

Resources

(handwritten note: ① Improve human resources)

The first main area where we need to improve our public affairs effort in the field concerns resources, especially human resources. In my current position in Cairo, I supervise, directly or indirectly, several million dollars in program resources, including ten Americans and about forty local staff. "Total PAO resources"—to use an old U.S. Information Agency term—to address the public diplomacy challenges we face here in Egypt would appear, on the surface at least, to be ample. In fact, numbers alone cannot tell the whole story.

Prior to 1999, our embassy PAOs were Foreign Service employees of the independent United States Information Agency (USIA), initially a creature of the Cold War that had, over the years, established itself as the respected official agency of U.S. culture and information overseas. However, by 1999, when Congress directed the Department of State to absorb the USIA and its programs, the once-proud agency had already been greatly diminished by a decade of downsizing, hiring freezes, and budget cuts.

While program budgets can be restored (if not always absorbed) in a single fiscal year, restoring essential personnel takes more time, and we have significant losses to make up in this area. USIA had essentially stopped hiring by the mid-1990s, both for the Foreign Service and for Civil Service support positions. Where did all the PAOs go? Following the USIA-State Department consolidation, some veteran PAOs retired or resigned. Other experienced PAOs—now also known as public diplomacy (PD) officers, to distinguish their work from the domestically oriented public affairs (PA) function—stayed on following the consolidation, but sought refuge in familiar, nonoperational duties, such as recruiting and training. Still others deduced that staying too long in public diplomacy assignments would leave them vulnerable to "selection out" by the Foreign Service's "up or out" promotion system. Cultural officers, for example, now reduced to "sub-section" head status in the field, saw themselves—rightly or wrongly—as disadvantaged in competition for promotion with section head colleagues who supervised fewer staff and smaller budgets. Career counselors encouraged their PD clients to seek out non-PD assignments. State officers from the other "cones" (tracks) did not volunteer for PD assignments in sufficient numbers to replace them.

(handwritten note: impact of USIA merger on PAO hiring)

Restoring personnel is not just a matter of hiring well-qualified and motivated entry-level officers. We must also find ways to preserve and rebuild our PD officer corps at the middle and senior grades. As experienced public diplomacy officers from the PD cone began bidding on—and getting—non-PD jobs, including jobs as ambassadors, deputy chiefs of mission, and principal officers, fewer officers with PD experience were left to fill senior PD positions in the field and back at headquarters. For mid-grade PD positions, including heads of one-officer sections, the cupboard was bare. The hiring freezes of the 1990s left little option other than to assign new hires and less-experienced officers, along with rehired recent retirees, to fill key PAO positions. Finding an experienced PAO (who was not a retiree) at an African post quickly became the exception, not the rule.

Even in the crucially important Arab and Islamic worlds, PD jobs were—and still are—routinely underbid. Adding to this difficult situation, we now must also staff our huge new mission in Iraq. We simply do not have enough experienced people to fill our vacant PD positions, so we draw down our field staff even further. In Cairo, three of my ten American positions were vacant this past year to support temporary duty assignments to Iraq. On paper, I had ten officers. In reality, I had only seven.

I should also add a brief comment about administrative support. At the time of the USIA-State merger, PD administrative specialists at the larger posts were moved out of public affairs sections, and their positions were absorbed within the State Department. The heavy administrative burdens on field PAOs, however, continued to grow. These internal duties (budget, personnel, grants management, and internal reporting) now compete seriously with PAOs' programmatic and personal contact responsibilities. The number of PD officers on paper at a given post does not reflect the amount of time these officers truly have available for PD duties.

Managing the Information Flow

The second main area for improving public diplomacy relates to new communication technologies. Even if the Berlin Wall had not come down, even if the Soviet Union were still on the world's maps, and even if USIA had not been merged into the Department of State, the work of our field PAOs would still have changed dramatically over the past decade as a result of revolutionary changes in how we communicate: satellite television, the Internet, digital video conferencing, mobile telephones, and short text messaging (SMS).

Twenty years ago, when I delivered a newly translated U.S. government text to a newspaper editor abroad, there was no doubt that a welcome service was being rendered: the information was just not otherwise available. Today, when a prisoner abuse scandal breaks in Iraq, we see the photos first on the front pages of Middle Eastern papers, 6-8 hours ahead of the U.S. East Coast. When the U.S. Congress debates military aid to Egypt, editorials appear hours later in the Egyptian press, before any U.S. government material can be prepared and delivered. When a minor exhibit in a provincial city touches a sensitive subject, a PAO in an Arab capital can be instantly deluged with e-mails and phone calls from both private and public contacts back in Washington urging immediate action. Even in developing countries, Web sites, e-mail and SMS alerts are increasingly replacing the hand-delivered print packets of just a few years ago.

In the mid-1980s, I was embassy PAO in Baghdad when Saddam Hussein's security services intentionally severed international telephone lines during the Iran-Iraq war. My main communications link to USIA headquarters was a single, hand-typed telegram per week. In such an environment, it was not difficult for me to manage the flow of information to and from Washington and other posts in the region. Today, as PAO in Cairo, I typically receive 300-400 e-mails a day, plus phone calls, text messages, memos, letters, and embassy telegrams. The post's information resource center (formerly known as the U.S. Information Service library) sends up an additional wealth of data each day, culled from international and local Web sites. The press office sends in detailed summaries of local media reporting. The program support office sends in vouchers to sign, grants to approve, budgets to review, and personnel documents to endorse. The PAO is at the center of this information maelstrom, and managing the flow of information to and from the PAO's office is a major challenge. One local-hire American secretary is just not enough.

A judicious delegation of authority over some administrative matters to other PD officers is only a partial solution. Additional training on how to better harness available technologies is another part of the solution. Ultimately, though, we need to recreate security-cleared, American specialist positions to support our PD sections overseas and keep these positions appropriately filled. Our language-trained PAOs—and all PD officers assigned overseas—should not be chained to their offices and computer screens, as is too often the case today. They should be getting out and engaging our high-value audience targets. With the right mix of support staff in every PD section, PAOs should be better able to monitor the data flow and still get out of the office for all-important personal contact work. Support staff positions in the larger PD sections, lost during the budget cuts of the 1990s, must be restored.

Ultimately, however, busy PAOs will require more than just additional staff support and expanded training to effectively cope with new technology and the exponentially growing flood of information into their offices. Our PAOs, and our embassies as a whole, need to rethink how we are organized to do business. In the meantime, we must not allow our field PAOs to drown in internal processes.

A Troubled Takeover

The third and final main area of our public affairs effort that needs to be improved relates to how we are organized, both in the field and in Washington. If the crisis we now face in the Arab and Muslim worlds really is, primarily, a public relations problem, is it not curious that our front line public relations professionals—our embassy and consulate PAOs overseas—are being asked to address this crisis with less internal authority and autonomy than they ever had before? Although there has always been a healthy competition in our PD effort between short-term advocacy (informational) work and long-term relationship-building (cultural) work, the basic operational principle used to be that the field had the lead and headquarters provided the support. No longer.

Since 9/11, our PAOs in the Arab and Muslim regions, as elsewhere, have been pushed more and more by Washington bureaus to support headquarters initiatives, rather than to conceive and execute their own projects with Washington support. The focus has been increasingly on short-term advocacy, with short-term publicity projects pushed at the expense of proven, long-term relationship-building activities, such as academic exchanges and the promotion of institutional linkages.

Part of this change, of course, relates to the reorganization of U.S. foreign affairs agencies in 1999. The merger of the independent USIA into the Department of State, as refracted in countless major and minor implementing directives and bureaucratic reorganizations, has created systemic impediments within what had been a fairly effective U.S. international communications effort during the Cold War. Admittedly, even without the merger, the resource budget cuts at USIA during the 1990s, rapidly changing technology, and deeply unpopular U.S. policies would have made programming to the Arab and Muslim worlds a major challenge for PAOs, in any case. We still would have enjoyed some successes, and we still would have had some failures. The September 11 attacks would, most likely, still have happened. With the merger, however, we broke something that has yet to be repaired.

Since USIA's merger with the Department of State, diplomats within the Department have tended to view their PAOs as in-house staff rather than as the autonomous programmers they were under USIA. Within the State Department, PAOs are now staff, whose principal role is to assist policy officers with their internal and external communications. It has become more difficult for PAOs to spend time on conceiving and executing autonomous activities. For the half-century prior to the USIA-State merger, however, a PAO in the field represented not only a staff function, but also the line management of an independent agency charged with delivering program support to all U.S. government departments and agencies overseas.

As USIA/USIS line managers overseas, PAOs focused primarily on administering specific programs: Fulbright academic exchanges, the International Visitor Program, "Arts America" presentations, traveling exhibits, and so on. Chiefs of mission held their PAOs accountable for how well they could organize and deliver USIA program support to local mission goals, but PAOs reported primarily to their agency head in Washington. PAOs were evaluated for promotion primarily by their USIA superiors in Washington, operating with much more autonomy than they have today. Regional cooperation on program design and execution was much closer under the independent agency structure. Chiefs of mission, in turn, focused primarily on policy management and reporting, typically working more closely with their political and economic officers than with their PAOs. Public diplomacy was not a primary concern for most ambassadors.

All this ended in 1999 with USIA's absorption into the Department of State. Despite months of pre-merger negotiation and Congressional earmarks to preserve USIA's established programs, resource-hungry State Department bureaus quickly found ways to gobble up the unexpected bounty and carry on essentially as before. Public diplomacy officers were dispersed throughout the Department, assigned to a jumbled mix of their former duties along with traditional State Department public affairs work, such as clearing press guidance and drafting speeches. "Cultural differences" between the old agency and the new department were evident.

The Department of State corporate culture generally values the role of the negotiator over that of the program manager, the savvy poker player over the flamboyant impresario. The negotiator's role is to produce documents and to close deals. The programmer's role is to organize publicity and public events. While publicly welcoming the former USIA officers as colleagues, many State officers persisted in viewing them as technical specialists, whose principal role was to assist them, the real line managers, in carrying out the Department's core diplomatic mission, not to promote the "soft power" of cultural, intellectual, and artistic endeavors.[3] Public diplomacy, perceived by some as little more than media relations, became a wholly subordinate function. PAOs, line managers under USIA, became support staff after the merger.

---

3. Joseph S. Nye, "The Decline of America's Soft Power," *Foreign Affairs* 83, no. 3, May/June 2004.

Meanwhile, the former USIA's headquarters apparatus—its established and integrated management structure that had supported its field posts so effectively for a half century—was largely dismantled. Once-powerful area offices, which had coordinated the full gamut of USIA programming across broad geographic regions, became small offices with little influence, buried within State's regional bureaus. The agency's experienced management staff was dispersed throughout the Department. USIA's Educational and Cultural Affairs (ECA) and International Information Programs (IIP) bureaus were retained, but without strong organizational links to the field. International broadcasting was made completely independent of the expanded Department of State. Our international communications machinery was dismantled, and we had only just begun to work on reassembly when the attacks of September 11, 2001, appeared on our TV screens.

Following 9/11, PAOs struggled to respond to an ambiguous mission: should they give priority to becoming traditional diplomats, drafting press guidance, talking points, speeches, and op-eds, that is, short-term message management to address America's image abroad? Or should they, instead, work together, informally, around a divided chain of command to save those established programs and exchanges that had largely defined the work of PAOs through fifty years of ideological conflict with communism? Many PAOs have tried to do both. Many are still trying, but a great deal of effort is being wasted. The sooner we can reconcile the two cultures and realize the synergies envisioned at the time of the USIA-State merger, the sooner we can throw our full weight against the challenges we face in the world today.

Managing a Public Affairs Section in the Field After 9/ll

A PAO today operates more closely with the embassy or consulate than ever before. The head of a public affairs section is typically one of five State Department section heads; the others are political, economic, consular, and management. All report to the ambassador through a deputy chief of mission. All sections, to some extent, have a functional sponsor back in Washington. These sponsors are not all engaged to the same degree with field posts. Some, such as the Consular Affairs Bureau or the Bureau of Diplomatic Security, are closely engaged with the field. Others are less actively engaged.

In the wake of the USIA-State merger, the immediate emphasis was on establishing the primacy of ambassadors and regional bureaus over public diplomacy operations. Now, I believe the pendulum needs to swing back a bit so that the PD function's sponsor, the undersecretary for public diplomacy and public affairs, and the domestic bureaus assigned to the function (Public Affairs, Educational and Cultural Affairs, and International

Information Programs) can play a stronger role for the field posts in such areas as monitoring strategic planning, standardizing personnel procedures, allocating human and financial resources, and coordinating regional and inter-regional programs.

A strong program sponsor in Washington would also serve as an effective counterweight to the understandable temptation in the field to divert public diplomacy resources to other priorities. Embassies are busy places, and, despite Congressional earmarks, PD resources are now assigned directly to the Department of State. When the work piles up, a personal commitment to the PD mission does not automatically ensure that the cultural officer will not have to pitch in on non-cultural duties.

As already noted, a PAO today, whether in a large or a small PD section, spends much more time in the office on internal business than outside on personal contact work. Twenty years ago, the USIA desk officer supervised all communication to and from his or her field posts, and the PAOs spent most of their time out of the office. Nowadays, individual bureaus and offices both within the Department of State and from other U.S. government departments and agencies routinely contact PAOs and other PA staff directly, primarily via e-mail. A big part of a PAO's job today is keeping these communications in the proper channels and ensuring that individual program elements are working in concert toward established priorities. In Cairo, with fifty PD employees in five offices spread across two cities, I spend up to 25 percent of my time in staff meetings just within the section. Another 25 percent goes into coordinating with the front office and the other sections, including Country Team meetings, Emergency Action Committee meetings, Interagency program meetings, and the like. When I add the time needed to manage e-mails, cables, phone calls, and other correspondence, I am grateful to find the time for one substantive outside call per day.

When I do manage to escape from the confines of our well-fortified embassy, I find that the nature of contact work has changed a great deal over the years. In Cairo, most of the real contact work goes on at night, when there is more time for patient listening, detailed explanations, and serious conversation. During the day, the schedule is just too crowded.

Our contacts, in general, are also now much better informed than before, since basic news about American policies and personalities is more readily available, via satellite television, the Internet and other channels, even in underdeveloped countries. For example, when a summary of a recent poll showing negative Egyptian attitudes toward the United States appeared in my e-mail from the U.S. one morning, I had already seen a detailed report of its release in *al Ahram*.

Individual programs are also becoming more time-consuming and difficult to execute. For example, when I was PAO in Baghdad twenty years ago, we could process a routine International Visitor Program (IVP) grant and put a nominee on a plane to the United States in less than a week. When pressed, we could do it in a day. Today, with tightened visa and security procedures, it can easily take 2-3 months to process a program visitor, and sometimes they do not get processed at all. Routine exchange program nominations are now planned 18-24 months in advance, and the staff time required to process them has ballooned. Although still valuable, the IVP (now called the International Visitor Leadership Program) is much less the short-term, tactical tool it once was.

Another big change in how we conduct our PD work overseas is related to the heightened security around our offices. Not too many years ago, I could measure how well my day had gone by the number of dirty Turkish coffee cups littering my office at closing time. Today, entire days go by without any outside visitors at all to share the forgettable American coffee I brew myself each morning. When contacts do come to the embassy, if they forget their photo IDs, I have to meet them out on the street. Likewise, I must meet them outside if they do not want to surrender their cell phones.

With no U.S. cultural center in Cairo any longer (our library is now an "Information Resource Center" within the embassy compound, behind several lines of security and more focused on external "outreach" than on serving walk-in traffic), those of us living downtown increasingly use our homes or other sites away from the office to meet contacts, even during the day. In the evening, I have, on occasion, had more than one event going on at a time at my home: for example, a youth group reception in the yard and a book discussion in the living room. In earlier times, such programs would have been conducted at a USIS cultural center. The need for increased security is an accepted fact of life at our missions abroad, but so is our need to get out and engage our important contacts regularly, and face-to-face.

If the Ambassador Is Boss, Then PD Work Must Be Ambassadorial

I have argued for the need to complete the unfinished business of the 1999 USIA-State merger. That does not mean that I think we should go back to the days of an independent, international public affairs agency. Instead, we need to complete that merger by making it a two-way process; that is, by getting State Department diplomats to buy into the notion of public diplomacy.

In the pre-merger days of USIA, a PAO was required to submit an annual program plan to his or her chief of mission for approval. That was an effective mechanism for ensuring that local and regional public affairs messages, methods, and audiences were all in sync with the goals and objectives set out by individual ambassadors. Some sought to work closely with their USIS/public affairs sections throughout the year, while others were satisfied with an occasional report and general sign-off.

PAOs, meanwhile, received regular directives from USIA headquarters to coordinate regional program efforts that individual ambassadors could, but seldom did, veto.

Since 1999, however, ambassadors have had direct authority over their PD sections. Washington-based program elements—in theory, at least—can now only request post support, not command it. If a support office back in Washington wants a field post to initiate some

> NOT TOO MANY YEARS AGO, I COULD MEASURE HOW WELL MY DAY HAD GONE BY THE NUMBER OF DIRTY TURKISH COFFEE CUPS LITTERING MY OFFICE AT CLOSING TIME. TODAY, ENTIRE DAYS GO BY WITHOUT ANY OUTSIDE VISITORS AT ALL TO SHARE THE FORGETTABLE AMERICAN COFFEE I BREW MYSELF EACH MORNING.

activity, the tasking is supposed to come via a formal cable. Informal e-mail communications among individual PD officers are not supposed to be used for formal taskings. Those orders should come to PAOs only through their ambassadors.

However, many PAOs maintain informal relationships with long-time colleagues in program offices back in Washington, and professional courtesies are still often exchanged without formal tasking. This can put a PAO in a difficult situation, however, if his or her ambassador calls for extensive local support at the same time informal promises to a Washington colleague need to be kept.

Some State Department diplomats have argued that public diplomacy is, primarily, what they themselves do in public to deliver policy messages. On the information side, an ambassador, deputy chief of mission, or other senior embassy officer can be a highly effective spokesperson, if he or she is willing and able to engage the media and other audiences as often as needed to deliver the basic policy messages. On the cultural side, though, public diplomacy officers are sometimes left to labor on their own, as such activities are often viewed as not important enough for direct ambassadorial involvement.

Leadership Is Still Key

Veteran PAOs like to cite the importance of what legendary USIA director Edward R. Murrow once called "the last three feet," the intimacy of face-to-face communication. That is especially true in a PAO's dealings with local staff, those bilingual (or multilingual) individuals who act as our guides and counselors in unfamiliar situations.

Whether the local staff is newly hired (as in Baghdad today) or mostly savvy veterans (as in Cairo), they are always a PAO's first and primary audience. If they are not well informed and truly convinced of the message, no amount of expensive technology or fancy wordsmithing will make much difference. Senior local staffers can be—and typically are—every bit as well educated, hard working, idealistic, and committed to the PD mission as any American officer. Their respect and trust must be earned anew by every incoming PAO. Without it, he or she cannot accomplish very much.

General Patton supposedly said, "Never tell a soldier what to do. Rather, tell him what needs to be accomplished, and let him amaze you with his creativity." I remember this advice often in my dealings with local staff. Respect for local autonomy and initiative was one of the great strengths of our public diplomacy operations in the past. I argued this point recently at the "Arabic Media and Public Appearance Forum" at the University of Maryland.[4] The focus of the forum was on identifying the language skills most needed by our field PAOs, and there was considerable discussion there about how to improve PAO debating skills so that we might be more effective advocates on satellite television programs.

At this forum, I presented a contrarian's view that the presence or absence of debating skills is not a major issue for most PAOs, especially in the Arab world. In fact, we spend most of our time on relationship building: visiting institutions, listening to contacts, and organizing public events. The image of the PAO as a debating champion is simply not realistic.

Every day we receive from various Washington offices far more pages of carefully crafted (in English, of course) "talking points" and "guidance" than any of us could ever use in a month. While we all do our share of direct advocacy, the main communicators in any good PD shop are almost always the local staff. They set up our appointments, take our calls, and translate our correspondence. A PAO's first job is always to win over these key individuals with a basic vision.

Who we are, as individuals as well as collectively as a people, and especially as viewed in the traditional and historically focused Arab and Islamic worlds, really does speak louder than talking points from Washington. How attractive we make that basic vision to our local staff goes a long way toward motivating them to take heat for us from their compatriots and to keep us engaged with the right local audiences, at the

---

4. University of Maryland, Center for Advanced Study of Language, "Arabic Media and Public Appearance Forum," June 8-10, 2004.

right times, with the right messages and the most effective delivery. Local staffs do not define our messages for us—we do that, and it is important that we be physically present to interact with our key contacts as American officers—but our local colleagues make a huge difference in how well we can deliver our messages and in making sure there is the right someone there to listen to us when we do.

I believe that effectively leading our local public diplomacy staff in the field requires a special kind of commitment. A field PAO must function as a kind of secular missionary, "proselytizing" others to respect and adopt the basic tenets of our value system: democracy, free markets, and social tolerance. If this is the case, then our local staff must be our first converts. If they do not believe in us, it will be difficult, if not impossible, for them to believe in what we are saying, or to convince others to believe us.

Plans Are Often Worthless, but Planning Is Everything

Every PAO knows that message, audience, and resources must be clearly defined and communicated to the entire PA staff for effective communication to take place. Standardized Mission Performance Plans currently provide only a general thematic umbrella, but effective PAOs need more specific guidelines for themselves, for their staff, for other embassy sections, and for the front office. A large PA staff may consist of a cultural/program unit, a press/media unit, and a library/outreach unit, plus administrative support and branch posts. All need to work together for the public diplomacy effort to have maximum impact on its selected target audiences, but this cannot and will not happen without a detailed program plan, clear budget allocations, and a good audience database.

Although PA-specific planning requirements were largely dropped following the USIA-State merger, they are now gradually being reinstated, beginning with a 2004 requirement for an annual submission by every post of a basic "influence analysis" paper for its host country. Audience databases will then be organized according to these analyses. Standardized software and training support for these databases are also pending. Posts are also increasingly asked to identify and use quantifiable measures of success to track their achievement of specific program goals and objectives. In Cairo, we are working with local advertising and market research firms to obtain audience-tracking data to use in such reporting.

Making a Difference After 9/11

There have been many recent studies and reports about our overall public diplomacy effort, especially in the Arab and Islamic worlds, after 9/11. Many of these offer conflicting advice: to recreate USIA (or not), to improve

PD training (or not), to expand our international broadcasting (or not), to streamline our visa policies (or not), to reach out to "wider, younger, and deeper" audiences, to provide more grant funding to local reformers, to make better use of technology, to create new programs ... Most of this is well intended so far as it goes, but the real need is systemic. No short-term initiative will have any lasting impact if we do not also invest in improving our public diplomacy infrastructure. We certainly need to strengthen the direct links between programming elements in Washington and the field.

As for our response to the Arab and Muslim worlds after 9/11, there are long-term trends and developments in every society that need to be watched, studied, understood, and, when possible, influenced in a positive direction. The role of an embassy PAO has always been primarily that of a long-term actor, not as a short-term reactor. Good media relations help to keep the dialogue orderly and misinformation to a minimum, but the real difference comes in long-term relationship building, establishing and maintaining mutually beneficial ties upon which the welfare of the American people ultimately depends. That is the truest, most important role of an embassy PAO, before or after 9/11, in the Arab and Islamic worlds or anywhere else.

5. A History of VOA Arabic: A Half-Century of Service to the Nation and the Arab World

Alan L. Heil Jr.

> *With war possibly just hours away, Baghdad is an eerie blend of public grit and private desperation. As the Education Ministry announces plans for midyear exams, families pack children off to stay with rural relatives. Iraqis parrot the bellicose words of Saddam Hussein, then nervously tune in the Voice of America to find out what's really happening.*
>
> —Tony Horwitz and Geraldine Brooks, *Wall Street Journal*,
> January 15, 1991

> *How like a shooting star and its quick flashes man's life doth seem; once bright, then ashes.*
>
> —Isa Khalil Sabbagh, quoting a proverb in *As the Arabs Say*, 1983

In Middle East calendar terms, the half-century life of the Voice of America (VOA) Arabic Branch was a mere quick flash in time. But consider the tumultuous events between 1950 and 2002 and the service's substantive and journalistically sound response to these events: five regional wars...the Egyptian-Israeli landmark peace accords of Camp David...the Oslo agreement between Israel and the Palestinians...the tragic eruption of the second intifada and Israeli crackdown...and the September 11 attack on America.

Seven months after 9/11, VOA's Arabic Branch disappeared at a single stroke, virtually unnoticed in the U.S. foreign affairs community, Congress, or in the American media. On Friday, April 19, 2002, at 7:02 A.M., a terse note was issued on the main wire at the Voice of America headquarters in Washington, D.C. "Effective this weekend," the note said, "the programming currently being produced for the VOA Arabic Branch will cease and all programming in Arabic will be produced for MERN, the

Middle East Radio Network" (also known as Radio Sawa).[1] Less than nine hours later, VOA Arabic broadcaster and program host Badia Rifai signed off for the last time. The staff was under strict orders by Sawa management not to say an on-air "goodbye" or "thank you" to its listeners.[2]

Nor was there a word of recognition, a word of thanks, to a VOA Arabic staff that had worked its heart out for two generations. It had, in war and peace, sought to produce the most accurate, timely, objective, and comprehensive programming possible. Its goal was to reflect events in the world and America, and U.S. official views in a classic "full service" format that at one time attracted as many as 6–10 million regular listeners.[3]

VOA Arabic was replaced, at the height of the Intifada and Israel's razing of Palestinian cities and villages, by Sawa, a predominantly pop music and entertainment service designed to appeal to youths. Sawa management prohibited its staff from using VOA's carefully sourced central newsroom material. Britney Spears and her Arab world pop singing counterparts were "in." Programs reflecting the richness of America and the nation's post-9/11 policy debates were "out." In the words of University of Michigan Middle East specialist Juan Cole: "The Arabic Service of the Voice of America used to be among the best and most extensive providers of news and discussion programs in the Arab world. To abolish it after September 11 and as the U.S. occupied Iraq boggles the mind."[4]

This chapter will briefly summarize the history of VOA Arabic from its first broadcast on January 1, 1950, until the last direct, over-the-air transmission of April 19, 2002. The account can be divided into five periods:

1. The Beginnings (1950-1962)
2. The Rhodes Years (1963-1977)
3. The Era of Renaissance (1978-1989)
4. The Gulf War: A Case Study (1990-1991)
5. The Twilight Years (1992-2002)

The Beginnings (1950-1962)

The Voice of America actually first went on the air in Arabic shortly after the network's first broadcasts on February 25, 1942.[5] The World War II

1. International Broadcasting Bureau (IBB) Notices, Friday, April 19, 2002, 7:02 A.M.

2. VOA Arabic staff members, interviews with author, August 12–15, 2002.

3. VOA Arabic Branch program review notes, June 18, 1985, 1.

4. Juan Cole, Informed Comment column, "Television Images Winning the Media War," May 5, 2004. www.juancole.com.

5. Robert William Pirsein, "The Voice of America: A History of the International Broadcasting Activities of the United States Government, 1940-1962" (Ph.D. dissertation, Northwestern University, Evanston, Illinois, June 1970), 70.

transmissions in Arabic were generally brief (fifteen minutes in length) and largely devoted to war news. After the Allied invasion of North Africa in November 1942, some VOA Arabic feeds were relayed by a program unit located in Algiers.[6] But the fledgling Arabic service was terminated in early 1945, when the defeat of Nazi Germany appeared imminent. When the war ended, VOA was cut further, from more than forty language services to twenty-three, from 1,167 hours to 446 hours a week.[7] For more than two years after the war, there were questions about the need, in peacetime, for broadcasting or, in fact, for any United States overseas information and cultural activities.

The Cold War changed all that. On January 27, 1948, Congress passed and President Truman signed the United States Information and Educational Exchange Act, better known as the Smith-Mundt Act (Public Law 402). The public diplomacy programs were revived, and, over the next several years, expanded to meet the challenges posed by the Soviet Union and the new Communist rulers of China. Broadcast languages were restarted or enhanced, approaching the World War II peak.

On January 1, 1950, veteran BBC commentator and analyst Isa Khalil Sabbagh, who had joined VOA, went on the air as the first voice of the new VOA Arabic Service. Years later, he cited the Voice's commitment to its listeners in the first broadcast: "The news may be good. The news may be bad. But we shall tell you the truth." In Sabbagh's words: "I cannot emphasize enough the business of truth. You cannot tell a lie and say that people are not going to notice or they don't understand a thing."[8]

Initially, VOA Arabic was on the air half an hour a day. But through the 1950s, the service grew rapidly. It was among the first language services at the Voice to broadcast English lessons. It gained momentum especially during the Suez crisis in 1956 (it surged then to fourteen and a half hours daily) and the landing of U.S. Marines in Lebanon in 1958. In each of these situations, White House and State Department pronouncements were translated and beamed in Arabic to the Middle East within minutes, a vital public diplomacy service. By 1958, VOA Arabic had increased to six hours daily, nearly matching the flagship English service.[9]

A distinguishing feature of the early Arabic service was its reflection of Arab culture and society to draw listeners to programming about the United

---

6. Ibid., 76.

7. Alan L. Heil Jr., *Voice of America: A History* (New York: Columbia University Press, 2003), 46.

8. Mohammed Dourrachad, "Arabic Service," VOA 50th anniversary profile, script No. 3-11372 (author's collection), 1, 5.

9. Pirsein, 358, 361, 405.

States and American policies. VOA Arabic program centers were established in Cairo in 1951 and in Beirut in 1955. They interviewed prominent writers, singers, entertainers, and historians and transmitted the materials back to Washington for rebroadcast. Initially, these centers concentrated almost exclusively on "soft" programming of a non-political nature, and guests included such legendary figures as singers Fairouz, Abdel Halim al Hafez, Abdul Wahhab, and Lebanese writer and historian Said Akl.

The program center staffs were flexible, however. Veteran VOA Arabic Branch broadcaster Ghassan Sabbagh recalls a cooperative arrangement with Radio Lebanon during the Marine landing of 1958. Then, he assisted in preparation and reading of the 1 P.M. prime time newscast for that national network in the VOA Arabic program center at the American embassy in Beirut.[10] Ghassan Sabbagh, who was Isa's younger brother, went on to become acting chief of the entire 45-member Arabic Branch in Washington before retiring in 2001.

Back in Washington in the late 1950s, change was in the air. VOA Director Henry Loomis and Program Manager Barry Zorthian were determined to make the Voice competitive globally as a respected source of news and programming. The market for small, inexpensive transistor radios was growing significantly in Africa, Asia, Latin America, and the Middle East. Loomis and Zorthian wanted to reach the new audiences there, as well as those behind the Iron Curtain. They felt that a statement of principles guiding VOA programming was essential to centralizing it and maintaining high-quality content.

Loomis, Zorthian, and others drafted the VOA charter asserting that it is in the long-range interests of the United States to communicate directly with the peoples of the world by radio. To be effective, the charter says, VOA must win the attention and respect of listeners. Its three operative paragraphs are:

(1) VOA will serve as a consistently reliable and authoritative source of news. VOA news will be accurate, objective, and comprehensive.

(2) VOA will represent America, not any single segment of American society, and will therefore present a balanced and comprehensive projection of American thought and institutions.

(3) VOA will present the policies of the United States clearly and effectively, and will also present responsible discussion and opinions on those policies.

---

10. Ghassan Sabbagh, interview with author, August 18, 2004.

The charter, originally published as a directive to the Voice during the final year of the Eisenhower Administration, eventually became law in 1976. The charter—and innovative technology—signaled striking changes in VOA Arabic programming and reach in the 1960s and 1970s.

The Rhodes Years (1963-1977)

Two likenesses of deer stand guard on each side of the entrance to the main harbor of the Greek island of Rhodes. Residents say these are where the legendary Colossus of Rhodes once stood, its two legs astride the harbor forming an archway over its entrance where ships sailed in ancient times. Beginning in 1952, a United States Coast Guard cutter, the *USS Courier*, was moored only a few hundred yards away from this spot, with a very modern mission. That was to relay Voice of America broadcasts in sixteen languages, including Arabic, to a vast slice of the planet, from the Soviet Union to Egypt, from Iran to North Africa, from central Europe to eastern Turkey.

The *Courier* was fitted with three transmitters, one 150 kilowatt medium wave, and two 35 kilowatt shortwave transmitters. They were directed initially by a balloon hoisted above the ship by its crew of eighty.[11] The vessel was ideal in the 1950s and early 1960s for VOA Arabic. That service needed a "close in" base for reaching the Levant and Egypt. The medium-wave (standard AM) transmissions were better, technically, than often fading, long-distance shortwave, especially for music programs. Moreover, an Arabic-speaking staff would be delivering the program at near "real time"; that is, no more than a time zone or two removed from its prime audience.

Program Manager Zorthian said that the *Courier* arrangement was temporary, pending conclusion of an agreement with the Greek government to build a land-based relay station on Rhodes. The Coast Guard cutter was very expensive to operate, and its last broadcast was in May 1964. By then, the Rhodes Relay Station had been built, and VOA Arabic staff began broadcasting from land rather than sometimes choppy seas. Nearly the entire VOA Arabic staff was moved from Washington to the eastern Mediterranean for direct broadcasts from a new program center at Koskinou, Rhodes. All news material was still edited and cleared in Washington.[12]

---

11. David Newell and Martin Manning, "The Voice of America in the Aegean: The Story Behind the First Floating VOA Radio Station, the Coast Guard Cutter 'Courier,'" *USIA World*, October/November 1989, 8-11.

12. Barry Zorthian, interview with author, August 18, 2004.

Blake Cochran, a veteran VOA manager, was named the first director of the Rhodes Program Center, and he joined Near East and South Asia Division director M. William Haratunian in Washington in transforming the Arabic Service. It became a full-fledged Branch, on the air seven hours daily.[13]   Haratunian reorganized the Cairo and Beirut program centers, re-designating them as subcenters of Rhodes.   He worked out the elaborate technical arrangements enabling them to report directly to both Rhodes and Washington.   Their journalistic and feature writing capabilities were greatly enhanced to serve both the Arabic and worldwide English services of the Voice. They also promoted VOA Arabic program placement and promotion.

The range of programming produced by the subcenters is described in my reports as well as those by Beirut Subcenter Director Frank Cummins. I headed the Beirut office in 1965–1966 and the Cairo subcenter in 1966 until the Arab-Israeli war the following June forced its closure.   Cummins, who directed the Beirut office from 1966-1969, described how news reports we wrote in English (which were then rendered in Arabic by our staff) were cleared in Washington for subsequent rebroadcast in Arabic by Rhodes:

> Topical news reports are cabled daily by the subcenter through the Embassy's telecommunications facilities to both VOA Rhodes and VOA Washington.   There is a daily radio-telephone circuit between Beirut and Rhodes (at 2:30 local time, Monday through Friday) over which voiced Arabic versions of the English reports are fed…Additional circuits can be ordered in the event of a major breaking story…[14]

Cummins went on to explain that Washington policy officers then reviewed the incoming English texts and determined their suitability for broadcast in one or both languages.   A teletype message was then sent to Rhodes indicating clearance or non-clearance. (This cumbersome system, designed forty years ago to ensure Washington control of the subcenters' politically sensitive output, would never be acceptable to U.S. government international broadcasters or executives in this era of high-speed digital communications, either for journalistic or technical reasons. Decisions on content at VOA today, with the exception of the U.S. government editorial, are made solely by professional staff journalists, not policy officers.)

The Beirut and Cairo subcenters produced hundreds of interviews and correspondent reports each year, from political reportage to human interest

---

13. Barbara L. Schiele, "VOA Broadcast Hours History," April 1973 (author's collection), 1.

14. Frank Cummins, "Beirut Subcenter," 1968, Beirut, Lebanon (author's collection), 6.

stories. After the June war, Beirut under Cummins' leadership carried the entire load and filed eight hundred topical reports in 1968 alone. Examples of feature programs and spots produced in the subcenters included *Spotlight on an Artist* (American as well as Arab), *American Short Stories* (multi-actor dramatizations of works by Twain, Hawthorne, Poe and others by master producer Mohammed Ghuneim in Beirut), *Book Reviews, Arabic Music Request, Western Music Request, Jazz Club USA, Do You Have a Question?* (listeners' queries about life in the United States researched and answered by subcenter staffs), and *Science Report.*

For the *Science Report*, the Cairo subcenter was aboard the *USS Oceanographer* for a transit of the Suez Canal about two weeks before the June war, and was able not only to interview American and Egyptian scientists but also to report the movement of Egyptian troops into the Sinai on the eve of the conflict.[15] During the war, telephone and booked broadcast circuits were severed by Egyptian authorities. Fifteen reports and dispatches were filed that week via embassy communications, some prepared via candlelight in blackout conditions. At noon on the fifth day of the war, telephone circuits temporarily opened up, and the subcenter filed reports on continuing fighting between Arab and Israeli forces on two fronts, latest battle news from the Suez Canal and Golan Heights, plans by President Nasser to address the nation, and the imminent evacuation of Americans from Egypt.

In the late 1960s and early 1970s, USIA Foreign Service Officer Richard Curtiss provided superb, area-savvy management at the Rhodes Program Center. Curtiss recruited more than a dozen stringers (contract reporters) in more than half of the twenty-two Arab countries. He expanded features originations on Rhodes and presided over VOA Arabic coverage of the Jordan civil war and the death of Nasser, both in 1970.[16]

The 1973 Yom Kippur War and its aftermath sorely tested VOA Arabic, and set in motion a series of American diplomatic moves that eventually led, under the Carter Administration, to the Camp David accords and the signing of a peace treaty between Egypt and Israel. The Rhodes Program Center continued, during most of the 1970s, to broadcast all VOA programs in Arabic, which expanded to seven and a half hours daily in 1977.[17] That was a year of profound change for the service.

---

15. Ibid., Alan L. Heil Jr., "Report of Activities, Cairo Subcenter," June 15, 1967, 1, 4, 7.

16. Curtiss later was Near East area director of the USIA, and on his retirement became executive editor of the *Washington Report on Middle East Affairs.*

17. Schiele, 6.

By the mid-1970s, it had become possible to transmit programs with crystal-clear audibility from Washington to distant regions via satellite. Until then, most Washington-originated programs had been delivered via shortwave (or on tape to Rhodes to avoid the adverse impact of shortwave transmission on music.) By 1977, the signal had improved so much that high quality programming—including music—could be satellite-fed from Washington to the Rhodes Relay Station. And it was a lot less expensive to maintain a programming staff in Washington than on Rhodes. Moreover, the outbreak of the Lebanese civil war in 1975 had caused the Beirut subcenter to close.

The entire Arabic Branch staff was transferred to Washington in 1977, including some of the more talented former members of the Beirut and Cairo subcenters who had moved to Rhodes. Rhodes staff members who had originally worked at VOA headquarters near the U.S. Capitol fourteen years earlier returned to a much-changed network. The charter (Public Law 94-350) had been signed by President Ford on July 12, 1976, very much resembling the executive order issued in 1960 but adding considerable weight to the practice of journalism at VOA. More staff effort could be focused on reflecting the United States, which for some, was their new adopted country.

There were disadvantages in the move, however. The staff was no longer broadcasting in "near real time" to its audience, which now was five to eight time zones ahead of Washington. Nor could staff members as easily travel home and absorb the latest nuances in language and culture which had kept their programming uniquely fresh since 1964. On the other hand, new reportorial opportunities were beginning to surface, with the revival of a Cairo office for VOA Arabic and the opening of a bureau headed by a VOA Arabic reporter in Amman.

The Era of Renaissance (1978-1989)

President Sadat's historic visit to Jerusalem had led to negotiations between Israel and Egypt that ended in the Camp David peace accord between Israel and Egypt in 1978. Former VOA Beirut subcenter veteran Mohammed Ghuneim was accredited to the marathon final round of talks among Presidents Carter, Sadat, and Israeli Prime Minister Begin at Camp David. The Arabic Branch deputy chief at the time, Salman Hilmy, recalls:

> Ghuneim provided full, hour by hour coverage from Camp David at the foot of the Catoctins. In addition to this coverage and sending voice actualities from the press center, Mohammed did several color pieces and two-ways with program hosts in the studio. The service also broadcast

a wide range of other material: U.S. and foreign media comment, both positive and negative reaction from around the world (much of the Arab world was quite critical of the Camp David talks at the time), backgrounders, opinion pieces and interviews with experts [Middle East specialists].[18]

In early 1982, I undertook a survey of all Voice language broadcast services that helped stimulate some much-needed reforms, not just in the Arabic Branch but throughout VOA. The broadcasters reached agreement on some basic new programming principles:

- VOA language services can become "reservoirs of creativity" if management is willing to encourage an atmosphere in which creativity can flourish.
- Regionalization, presence, and more service originations are essential to dynamic radio programming that speaks directly to listeners. (Until the early 1980s, much of the language service programming had been translations of English scripts written in the central news and current affairs divisions. Now, they were encouraged to develop reportage on their own, sharing it with the rest of VOA.)
- Too much programming (it was said at the time of the survey) has an automated sound, a sound of being rewritten or retranslated. Many more actualities (recorded or live voices) should be used to vary the programming.[19]

The survey findings were used to help set standards in program reviews and evaluation panels at the Voice. The study also applied to a newly constructed mobile studio called the Voyager. The vehicle traveled throughout the continental United States in 1985 and 1986 before budget cuts forced it off the road. VOA Arabic broadcasters Mohammed Shinnawi and Mounir Mohammed joined its crews for several weeks as it reflected life in such diverse places as the American southwest, Mount Rushmore, and Michigan, where the nation's largest Arab-American community lives. "A wealth of Americana material (from Voyager) was aired on our cultural programs," Hilmy recalls. "On several occasions, Arabic Branch reporters telephoned more timely items to Washington from important stopovers of the mobile studio."[20]

---

18. Salman Hilmy, e-mail interview with author, August 19, 2004.

19. Alan L. Heil Jr., "Survey of Broadcast Services on Program Development," March 23, 1982, 1-2.

20. Salman Hilmy, e-mail interview with author, August 19, 2004.

In 1985, VOA Arabic expanded its programming from seven and a half to nine and a half hours daily. A program review held May 28 that year described the media environment at the time:

> The Branch broadcasts to a population estimated at 180 million spreading eastward from Morocco across North Africa and three time zones to the Middle East and the Arabian Sea. Listening audiences and their spoken Arabic are diverse, as are their politics, culture and social structures. Linguistically, residents of Tunis and Cairo may not be able to converse in the local dialect of their respective countries. But they may communicate effectively in journalistic Arabic, which VOA uses to reach its widespread audience. The much larger challenge is how to program, what to broadcast to an audience in twenty-two countries, an audience made up of royalists and socialists, Bedouins and westernized urbanites, sheikhs and peasants and all classes in between. The task is made more difficult by the ambivalence with which the Arab world regards the United States. Listeners have a high regard for U.S. accomplishments in science and technology, space exploration, medicine, education and individual freedoms. But they harbor a dislike for America's apparent unquestioning support for Israel, its perceived lack of concern for Palestinian self-determination, and the impression of anti-Arab bias in the media and elsewhere.[21]

Speaking at the program review session, Salman Hilmy (who had been promoted to Arabic Branch chief) said that VOA Arabic could deal with such a diverse audience only by programming to all areas within the framework of the charter. He added that the perceived U.S. "tilt" toward Israel is countered through balanced and factual news programs that use authoritative official statements, better reporting of Arab-American activities, and U.S. media coverage of area-related issues. Hilmy said VOA Arabic chose topics for its Americana programs that demonstrated equality and open opportunity in U.S. society, especially through the experiences of Arabs and Muslims in this country. Because of the large number of young people in the Arab world, Hilmy concluded, the Branch had programs that deal with youth and education in America, as well as extremely popular music and English teaching programs.[22]

---

21. Arabic Program Review notes (Washington, DC: International Broadcasting Bureau, Office of Program Review), May 28, 1985.

22. Arabic Program Review notes (Washington, DC: International Broadcasting Bureau, Office of Program Review), June 26, 1986, 1-2.

The Gulf War: A Case Study (1990-1991)

The Arabic Branch met the greatest test of its sixty-two year history during the Persian Gulf crisis and war. That period lasted from August 2, 1990, as Iraqi armed forces occupied Kuwait until February 28, 1991, as coalition forces drove Saddam Hussein's army from the sheikhdom. There were challenges around the clock to get the news right, to get it quickly, and to report all U.S. or coalition official statements during the seven-month crisis.

The journalistic and public diplomacy aspects of the crisis were daunting. In the late 1980s, Mahmoud Zawawi had succeeded Hilmy as Arabic Branch chief, when the latter was promoted to chief of the Near East and South Asia Division overseeing Arabic and six other language services. "During the Gulf War," Zawawi said, "we exercised great caution because for the first time this conflict involved the United States against an Arab country, and it also divided Arabs among themselves. So we had to be as objective in our coverage as possible in order to maintain our credibility."[23]

Even before the crisis erupted, there was official U.S. pressure on Voice of America content. Just eight days prior to Saddam's invasion of Kuwait, the Department of State killed a draft U.S. government editorial written at Voice headquarters for broadcast by the VOA in Arabic, English, and other languages. The editorial noted that Iraq had massed "thousands of troops, as well as tanks and missiles, near its border with Kuwait. The U.S.," the draft said, "is concerned about the buildup of military forces along the Iraq-Kuwait border. U.S. officials have stressed that there is no place in a civilized world for coercion and intimidation."[24]

The State Department gave no official reason for killing the editorial. Washington, several press accounts speculated, was reluctant to criticize Saddam because it wanted to maintain good relations with Iraq. According to press accounts, timid official responses to Saddam's actions may have emboldened him to miscalculate the consequences of occupying Kuwait.[25] After the Iraqi invasion of Kuwait, however, American policy took a 180-degree turn.

A few hours after Iraq's attack on August 2, 1990, VOA Director of Programs Sid Davis authorized the first of three Arabic Branch schedule expansions. These ultimately reached fifteen and a half hours daily (with occasional specials pushing it to seventeen and a half hours.) The broadcasts

---

23. Dourrachad, 3-4.
24. "New Persian Gulf Threats," draft U.S. government editorial, July 25, 1990 (author's collection), 1.
25. Heil, 320-21.

were all-news and live. Repeat material was kept to a minimum. Arabic language correspondents or stringers filed reports from such diverse datelines as the White House, Congress, the United Nations, Riyadh, Taif, Manama, Damascus, Jerusalem, Amman, Cairo, Rabat, Nouakchott, and various European capitals, as well as Baghdad before Desert Storm and Kuwait on the day of liberation. The Arabic Branch aired more than two thousand interviews, reports, and program segments. There were eighty specials conveying to listeners full texts of U.S. and coalition statements. VOA Arabic also broadcast U.S. government editorials three times daily, and cancelled all music during hostilities. This was labor-intensive programming, much more responsive to audience information needs than the Radio Sawa pop music and headline service provided during the Iraq war of 2003.

The Arabic Branch news desk updated around-the-clock an automated dial-in telephone news service. That service, staff recordings of the latest crisis news, received more than seventy thousand calls between August 1990 and March 1, 1991. Moreover, VOA Arabic aired call-in programs and simultaneous interpretations of major events at all hours of the day or night. There were ninety-one such live programs, including Arabic simultaneous interpretations of news conferences by President Bush, U.N. Security Council sessions, and military briefings at the Pentagon and in Saudi Arabia. Prewar call-in programs featured ambassadors of the United States, Iraq, Kuwait, and Egypt.[26]

At the same time, VOA was subjected to unprecedented public scrutiny. About two weeks after Desert Storm began, allegations that VOA Arabic broadcasts had aided Saddam surfaced in U.S. dailies such as the *Wall Street Journal* and *New York Post*, and also on Capitol Hill. The USIA inspector general echoed some of the complaints months later. But independent experts cleared the Voice of charges that it had tilted toward Iraq. The allegations of bias stemmed from complaints in Cairo and Riyadh, where some high-ranking officials had expected VOA Arabic to follow journalistic standards typical of Middle East state-controlled media. Saudi media, for example, had not even reported the Iraqi invasion of Kuwait until more than seventy-two hours after it occurred. Coalition partners criticized Voice coverage of official statements from Baghdad.

At the request of VOA Director Richard Carlson and his deputy, Robert Coonrod, the Center for Strategic and International Studies (CSIS) in Washington, D.C., and the Hudson Institute of Indianapolis, Indiana, reviewed hundreds of hours of VOA Arabic programming during

---

26. Ibid., 322.

the conflict. Both agreed that VOA programming was "effective and responsible," as the Hudson Institute put it. The 205-page CSIS analysis concluded:

> By standard U.S. journalistic practice, VOA, at worst, made some questionable calls. The vast majority of its coverage, however, should be judged as clearly within the boundaries set by the U.S. journalistic canon. It would be wrong to suggest that its coverage was biased against the coalition forces or that it was an unwitting dupe of Saddam Hussein. Neither the qualitative assessment of VOA's overall thoroughness and balance by CSIS analysts, nor the quantitative analysis performed, leads to that conclusion.[27]

CSIS analyst Shireen Hunter, an Arabic speaking Middle East specialist, sketched the cultural context of U.S. Gulf War broadcasts to the region. Much of what she had to say remains relevant in the post-9/11 world:

> First, in the case of VOA, too one-sided or propagandistic-sounding broadcasting would probably undermine its credibility and thus its ability to make a gradual dent on some regional biases. Second, it is also clear that any dramatic change in VOA broadcasting standards in order to "get along" in the Middle East would be counterproductive. Indeed, it could lead to a significant drop in VOA's listenership by undermining its credibility. Third, given their skepticism and cynicism, Middle East listeners resort to various sources to get information. Thus, the non-inclusion of sensitive items in VOA broadcasts does not mean that news will not reach the Middle East. Indeed, it will, but possibly in a slanted and distorted form that would not be the case with VOA.[28]

The VOA program review and evaluation staff also tracked Arabic Branch logs and content day by day, during the crisis and for a month after the war ended. Based on minor lapses that occurred during those months, the internal Voice audit suggested improvements in VOA Arabic editorial controls. These were: (1) tighten editing of press roundups, (2) more rigorously review the content of field stringer reports, and (3) shorten and balance interviews to reflect all sides in a crisis or dispute.[29]

---

27. *Analysis of Voice of America Broadcasts to the Middle East During the Persian Gulf Crisis* (Washington, DC: Center for Strategic and International Studies, 1991), 53.
28. Ibid., 64.
29. Heil, 324-325.

VOA Arabic interviewed more than 760 Americans, Arabs, Europeans, and Israelis from August 1990 through February 1991. Among them were Admiral William Crowe; Middle East scholars Rashid Khalidi, Judith Kipper, Michael Hudson, and Gregory Gause; *New York Times* correspondent Yousef Ibrahim; Saudi Prince Mohammed Ibn Fahd; former U.S. Ambassadors James Akins and Edward Peck; former Undersecretary of State Joseph Sisco; former Assistant Secretaries of State Lucius Battle and Richard Murphy; former Senators George McGovern and Charles Percy; former U.N. Secretary General Boutros Boutros Ghali; Seeds of Peace founder John Wallach; Palestinian leader Saeb Erekat; Israeli scholar Moshe Sharon; Arab League envoy Clovis Maksoud; prominent Arab-American activist Khalil Jahshan; nationally syndicated U.S. radio host Casey Kasem; and public opinion survey specialist James Zogby.[30]

These exclusive interviews were broadcast on the Arabic Branch flagship program *Around the World* and in other programs around the clock. The field correspondents and contract reporters gave the Voice a competitive reach in covering the beginning of the air war, the Iraqi Scud missile attacks against Saudi Arabia and Israel, the launching of the ground war, and the mass surrender of Iraqi soldiers fleeing their bunkers as coalition forces moved rapidly northward.

This was the first Middle East war to be highlighted on television screens around the world, thanks to CNN. However, according to a USIA Office of Research memorandum, listening to foreign radio increased dramatically in four Gulf states surveyed during the crisis. VOA's regular (once a week) listening rate among Saudi adults increased from 12 to 19 percent. In the United Arab Emirates, the regular listening rate surged from 1 to 10 percent, and there were striking audience gains in Bahrain and Oman as well.[31]

Specialists on the region caution, however, that audience figures are only rough approximations. That is especially the case in the Middle East, where respondents in surveys often tell researchers what they want to hear, or confuse the many networks—local, regional, and international—available in an area where more external broadcasters compete than anywhere on earth. The fundamental question is: Who is listening and why? Is it those leaders who make a difference? Or is it those who seek merely to be entertained and are less interested in being informed?

---

30. VOA Arabic program logs, August 1990 through March 1991 (author's collection).

31. "Foreign Radio Listening Rates High in Four Arab Gulf Nations; VOA Increases Audience During Crisis," United States Information Agency Research Memorandum, Washington, DC, February 14, 1991, 1.

VOA Arabic got an unexpected answer to the question just three and a half months after Iraq invaded Kuwait in 1990.   On *ABC Prime Time Live*, anchor Peter Jennings had a rare interview with Saddam Hussein. It was the last the Iraqi leader would grant to an American network until 2002. Jennings later observed that the Iraqi leader seemed exceptionally well informed. He corrected an interpreter about the number of additional U.S. troops recently ordered to the region by President Bush. He was aware that Mr. Bush soon would be traveling to Saudi Arabia to visit American troops on Thanksgiving Day. Saddam's interpreter confided to Jennings that the Iraqi president had just come from listening to an Arabic evening broadcast of the Voice of America.[32]

On-scene reportage by experienced central newsroom and Arabic Branch correspondents may have been the most effective feature of VOA Arabic programming during 1990 and 1991. On the last day of the war, the Branch's senior correspondent Mohammed Ghuneim was among the first reporters to ride in an armored personnel carrier into a newly liberated Kuwait. Here are excerpts of Ghuneim's report:

> The unmistakable evidence of the ferocious war waged for Kuwait over the last few weeks is apparent with the first step across the Saudi-Kuwaiti border.   Bulldozers had erased the modern highways.   Trenches and minefields took their place...In Kuwait City, everything in sight was a grim reminder of the people's hunger, thirst, and suffering. Further proof came at noon, when a creeping cloud of smoke from burning oil wells eclipsed the sun and devoured the light. Fumbling through pockets and purses, passersby pulled out their battery-operated torches, if only to light the bleakness of the soul.   Suddenly, it rained, washing away the black veil...Daylight returned and with it, Kuwaitis went on to celebrate their freedom.[33]

The Twilight Years (1992-2002)

The Gulf War generated fresh diplomatic pressures for settlement of the Arab-Israeli dispute.   VOA Arabic, now in full flower, broadcast live the historic Madrid conference bringing Arab and Israeli delegates together for the first time in a public forum (October 1991) and the White House signing of the Oslo Peace Accords between Israel and the Palestinian Authority (September 1993).

---

32. Heil, 311.

33. Mohammed Ghuneim, correspondent report translated from Arabic, March 1, 1991 (author's collection).

The Branch produced a number of new features programs reflecting life in America. Old favorites such as the English lessons in Arabic were recast and brought up to date. Representative titles included: *Medicine Today, New Horizons in Science, Quills and Colors* (literature and arts in America and the Arab world), *Accent on Youth, Book World, Business Week,* and *Democracy in Action* (fundamentals of American civil society.) *Success Story* reflected the experience of immigrants, Arab and non-Arab. *Poet's Corner* and *Cross-Cultural Spotlight* examined modern Arab poetry and the history of literary interaction between the West and the Arab world.

In the post-Cold War period, on the other hand, there was talk of massive reductions of U.S. international broadcasting. The budgets of the larger networks, VOA and Radio Free Europe/Radio Liberty were cut substantially, even as smaller Radio Free Asia and Television Marti outlets were created. The net effect was to reduce annual expenditures for the Voice and its sister broadcasters from $450 million to about $300 million annually. During the decade before 9/11, little attention was paid to the Middle East. By 1994, VOA Arabic had been reduced from its Gulf War peak of fifteen and a half hours a day to seven and a half hours daily. It struggled to compete in an increasingly crowded marketplace of ideas.

A program review summary in late 1992 reflected growing concern on the part of both VOA management and broadcasters. "One of VOA's finest large services, the Arabic Branch, broadcasts to an important and still potentially dangerous region," the review document said,

> With diminishing resources, the Branch is struggling to hold its listenership against increasing competition from more than a score of other international radios, from international Arabic-language television operations like that being mounted by the BBC, and from a growing number of Arab-owned commercial radios. Despite the high quality of its programs and the importance of its audience, VOA Arabic is severely handicapped by not having a competitive radio signal in much of the Arab world. USIA-commissioned research indicates VOA urban listenership has declined in four of five countries recently surveyed (Egypt, Jordan, Lebanon, Saudi Arabia, and the United Arab Emirates). With little prospect for substantial placement on regional stations, it is imperative that the VOA Arabic signal be improved. Meanwhile, the Branch should continue to reexamine and redefine its programming in light of the Arab world's changing media environment.[34]

---

34. Frank Cummins, "VOA Arabic Branch Program Review Notes," October 20, 1994 (author's collection).

VOA attempted to meet the technical and programming challenges: On January 5, 1996, it joined with Worldnet Television and the most-watched Arabic television network at the time, the Saudi privately owned Middle East Broadcasting Centre (MBC) in London, to co-produce a weekly hour-long call-in program, *Dialogue With the West*. Early guests included U.S. Assistant Secretary of State for Human Rights and Humanitarian Affairs John Shattuck; Assistant Secretary of State for Near East Affairs Robert Pelletreau; Syrian Foreign Minister Farouk al Sharaa; and Saudi Deputy Oil Minister Prince Abdul Aziz Bin Salman. The

> BY 1994, VOA ARABIC HAD BEEN REDUCED FROM ITS GULF WAR PEAK OF FIFTEEN AND A HALF HOURS A DAY TO SEVEN AND A HALF HOURS DAILY. IT STRUGGLED TO COMPETE IN AN INCREASINGLY CROWDED MARKETPLACE OF IDEAS.

program was rebroadcast by VOA Arabic on radio.

In the spring of 1996, VOA's Kuwait medium-wave transmitter was enhanced greatly, with its power increased from 100 to 600 kilowatts. VOA's signal into Iraq, Iran, and several of the Gulf emirates was considerably strengthened. At the same time, the Office of Engineering began work on upgrading the long-established Rhodes medium-wave transmitter from 300 to 600 kilowatts. This would strengthen VOA's reach in Arabic and English to the Levant and the populous Nile Delta. By 1996, the Branch's dial-in recorded news service (retained after the Gulf War) had received more than a quarter of a million calls.

The resources available to take advantage of these new facilities continued to evaporate, despite rapid changes in the media environment in the Arab Middle East that required new investment. *Dialogue With the West* was plagued by coordination problems between Washington and London; it lasted just under two years. BBC Arabic TV closed down after a dispute over content with its Saudi-financed satellite carrier, Orbit. Many of the BBC staff emigrated to Qatar and formed the core of what was to become a formidable force in the region and beyond, al Jazeera TV. Indigenous satellite TV, in the next decade, was to transform Middle East media and politics, as al Jazeera and MBC's affiliated service, al Arabiya, were to prove after 9/11 and during and after the Iraq war.

At VOA, the first wave of staff cuts occurred in 1996, heavily reducing language services to eastern and central Europe but deeply affecting other services as well. A Voice-wide hiring freeze prevented filling vacancies in the Arabic Branch, now down to about four-fifths of its size at the time of the Gulf War. Nonetheless, the Branch continued to maintain its Cairo and Amman offices and had stringers in Jerusalem, Damascus, Rabat, Algiers,

Tunis, Manama, Kuwait, Vienna, and Tuzla (Bosnia.) By 2002, the Arabic Branch full-time staff had shrunk to around thirty, compared with the 1990 level of fifty.

A program review on March 29, 2000, praised the Branch's live coverage of the unsuccessful Israeli-Syrian talks in Shepherdstown, West Virginia, its field reportage on Israel's withdrawal from southern Lebanon, and its programming on the death of Syrian President Hafez al Assad and accession of his son Bashar to the Syrian presidency. In covering the Syrian transition, VOA Arabic was able once again to bring to its microphones a wide array of expert observers, among them Moroccan Foreign Minister Ben Alissa, former Egyptian Prime Minister Mustafa Khalil, and former American diplomat Robert Pelletreau.

But audiences for international radio networks broadcasting to the Arab world declined significantly from 1995 to 2000 as use of FM and satellite TV soared.

According to a study ordered by the U.S. Broadcasting Board of Governors (BBG) and frequently cited by it, the VOA Arabic weekly adult audience at the turn of the century was about 2 percent of the adult population. Yet BBG press releases failed to mention other findings: (1) VOA's high-quality audience, though small, had remained steady as other international radio broadcasters lost listeners between 1995 and 2000; and (2) VOA Arabic was judged by those surveyed to have had the "best network of international correspondents" and "best analysis" of current events.

This was an asset VOA management was determined to preserve and strengthen, even before September 11, 2001. At the end of 2000, Near East Division Director Ismail Dahiyat and Program Director Myrna Whitworth worked overtime through the year-end holidays, in collaboration with VOA engineers and outside experts, to come up with a comprehensive blueprint for building a substantively solid, competitive Arabic Branch. The $15 million plan would have expanded VOA Arabic to an around-the-clock service with FM leases in a number of urban population centers, with greatly enhanced medium-wave facilities (Cyprus, Kuwait and/or Abu Dhabi) and a three-hour block of high quality television as part of a 24-hour Arabic/English stream. The plan called for a VOA Arabic schedule consisting of youth-oriented programs, including music, but with conflict resolution, dialogue and interview programs as well as solid news and analysis. The intended audience was clearly identified as "young Arabic-speaking people, future and current decision makers, and those who may eventually play a role in a peaceful resolution of the Middle East crisis." VOA Director Sanford J. Ungar submitted the proposal to the Middle East subcommittee of the BBG on January 4, 2002. That was just nine months before 9/11 and only a few weeks after Norman J. Pattiz of Westwood One, nominated by President Clinton, had joined the BBG. The Board rejected the VOA proposals almost immediately, saying: "We're not going to do it that way."[35] The die was cast for the twilight months of VOA Arabic.

Looking back, VOA Arabic had engineering and promotional support which paled in comparison to that later provided to Radio Sawa and Alhurra TV. Sawa today has FM relays in a dozen Arab countries, and greatly enhanced medium-wave delivery systems. Alhurra is on the best region-wide satellite distribution carriers. The final year's investment in VOA Arabic: $4.5 million. The first year's investment in Radio Sawa: $35 million. The first year's investment in Alhurra: $102 million.[36] Middle East scholar Juan Cole recently asked why VOA Arabic had not been sustained on FM in Iraq (as the Whitworth-Dahiyat blueprint would have ensured) instead of Sawa, predominantly pop music.

The Arabic Branch was tested significantly one last time during the 9/11 tragedy. VOA Arabic, along with VOA's more than fifty other language services, shifted to an all-news format within moments after the World Trade Center and Pentagon were attacked. Near East Division Director Ismail Dahiyat recalls:

> Almost immediately, VOA Arabic broadcasts were increased to eleven hours daily, and remained that way until a few months before closure of the service. More than in any previous crisis, we focused on multimedia (TV and the Internet) as well as radio. We established a weekly TV call-in program, *Hello America*. And our Web site expanded greatly, drawing several hundred thousand visits each month.[37]

Traffic on the VOA Arabic Web site more than doubled the week of September 11–18, 2001.[38] The Branch broadcast simultaneous

---

35. Myrna Whitworth, e-mails to author, August 26, 2004; Ismail Dahiyat, interview with author, August 25, 2004. VOA drafted a second, more modest $2.3 million enhancement plan. It focused on strengthening radio, TV, and Internet offerings, three FM leases, and a simulcast radio-TV call-in modeled on the highly successful Arabic Brach radio call-in, *Hello America*. That plan was never submitted because the Board remained committed to an entirely different approach.

36. For the VOA final budget, see BBG budget submission for FY 01 and FY 02; for Radio Sawa costs, see BBG Fact Sheet, September 23, 2003, 2; for Alhurra figures, see BBG Fact Sheet "Alhurra Television," April 27, 2004. "Recent Research on VOA Arabic," presentation to the BBG, January 2001, prepared by the Office of Research, International Broadcasting Bureau: Washington, DC.

37. Ismail Dahiyat, interview with author, August 22, 2004.

38. Heil, 409.

interpretations of statements by President Bush and his secretaries of state and defense as the United States sought to build a global coalition against terrorism.   VOA Arabic assisted Worldnet television with special video reports.

Overnight, there was a renewed strategic need for the Voice of America to offer in-depth news and analysis of the terrorist threat in the Arabic language, for serious reporting and discussion of this new plague on humanity.   Instead, six months after 9/11, undreamed of new resources were obtained and invested in Radio Sawa, largely entertainment-driven and completely divorced from VOA.   An effort to revive a VOA Arabic Web site in January 2003 was stillborn; it offered multi-faceted glimpses at the Iraq war, United States policies, and the richness of life in America, and it was popular with editors, educators, and other intellectuals.   Yet it vanished on April 15, 2004, for lack of BBG support.   The disappearance of VOA Arabic at a time when it was needed most ranks among the great tragedies in the history of U.S. international broadcasting.

6. Radio Sawa and Alhurra TV: Opening Channels of Mass Communication in the Middle East

Norman J. Pattiz

[The terrorists] know that a vibrant, successful democracy at the heart of the Middle East will discredit their radical ideology of hate. They know that men and women with hope, and purpose, and dignity do not strap bombs on their bodies and kill the innocent. The terrorists are fighting freedom with all their cunning and cruelty because freedom is their greatest fear.

—President George W. Bush

On September 11, 2001, the United States had no significant channels of mass communication with the people of the Middle East. Today, with the new broadcasting initiatives of Radio Sawa and Alhurra TV, we do. Three years ago, our only broadcast link, the Voice of America's Arabic-language radio service, was attracting a measured weekly audience of roughly two million adults in the region. Today, Sawa and Alhurra have a total unduplicated weekly audience of some 24 million Arab adults (and likely millions more in countries not yet surveyed), as measured by ACNielsen studies and other research in July and August 2004 in eight Middle Eastern countries.

Multiple waves of survey research in the Middle East in the last several years confirm sustained weekly audiences for Sawa and Alhurra, suggesting they are becoming part of Arabs' regular media mix. This is a remarkable finding given Arabs' dislike of the United States and U.S. policy, and it points to Sawa and Alhurra's staying power and prolonged impact. Moreover, the research shows that large percentages of these weekly audiences find the stations' news to be reliable.

It is true, but hardly surprising, that Arabs turn first to al Jazeera, al Arabiya, and other indigenous sources for news instead of U.S.-supported channels. However, the issue for Sawa and Alhurra is not whether Arabs use them for news first but whether they use them for news at all. And they do. Arab audiences, like people everywhere, typically consult multiple sources for news and information.

By regularly reaching unprecedented numbers of Arabs with accurate and balanced reporting, current affairs programs, debates, roundtables, interviews with U.S. policymakers, and much more, Sawa and Alhurra are making a vital contribution to long-term U.S. foreign policy goals of promoting freedom and democracy in the region. For, without an informed citizenry, there is no chance for democracy.

The Broadcasting Board of Governors

Sawa and Alhurra are model initiatives of the Broadcasting Board of Governors (BBG), the federal agency responsible for all non-military international broadcasting funded by the U.S. government.[1]

The Board is bipartisan with four Republicans, four Democrats, and the Secretary of State as an *ex officio* member. Together they constitute a collective chief executive officer. Each member is appointed by the president and confirmed by the U.S. Senate. Each has one vote in agency decisions.

The Board's responsibilities encompass strategic planning, budgetary and legal affairs, intra-governmental relations, and oversight to ensure adherence to mandated standards and principles. Among key Board duties are serving as a firewall against interference in news content and reviewing annually all BBG language services to adapt broadcasting to global media and political developments, deleting and adding services as necessary.

These latter functions go to the heart of why Congress originally created the Board and later established all of U.S. international broadcasting as an independent federal agency. Only an independent board of directors made up of private citizens with experience in broadcasting and governmental affairs has the wherewithal to ward off interference with journalistic content and to spark change within the bureaucracy.

The BBG's team of broadcasters includes the long-established Voice of America (VOA), Radio Free Europe/Radio Liberty (RFE/RL), Radio

---

1. The BBG was established in 1994 by the U.S. International Broadcasting Act as an autonomous body, operating in conjunction with the now-defunct United States Information Agency (USIA). The 1998 Foreign Affairs Reform and Restructuring Act abolished USIA and transferred most of its functions into the Department of State. The BBG became an independent federal agency. The name "Broadcasting Board of Governors," which previously had referred only to the nine-member board, became the name of the new agency. In this chapter, "BBG" will refer to the agency as a whole; "Board" will denote the nine-member board that provides leadership for the agency.

Free Asia (RFA), and Radio and TV Martí, as well as new broadcasters like Sawa and Alhurra (including Alhurra-Iraq), under the umbrella of the Middle East Television Network. These broadcasters have different legal frameworks—some are federal entities, others are grantee organizations—but all adhere to the same code of journalistic standards as set out in the U.S. International Broadcasting Act.

This same legislation, together with the 1998 Foreign Affairs Reform and Restructuring Act, constitutes the basis for the BBG mission: "To promote and sustain freedom and democracy by broadcasting accurate and objective news and information about America and the world to audiences overseas." This was, in essence, VOA's mission in the face of Nazism during World War II and RFE/RL's mission in the face of Soviet totalitarianism during the Cold War. And today, it is Sawa and Alhurra's mission in the face of radical Islamic fundamentalism in the war on terror.

It is unrealistic to think we can accomplish this mission overnight. Receptivity to BBG broadcasts in the Middle East is strongly affected by negative Arab perceptions of U.S. policy in the region. In the face of this animosity, our role is to exemplify a free press in action. We let the facts speak for themselves. We are confident that our overseas audiences, once fully informed, will make decisions that over the long run will coincide with U.S. values and interests—with what President Bush has called a "forward strategy of freedom."

Therein lies the BBG's unique contribution to public diplomacy, the business of engaging, informing, and influencing overseas audiences about the United States and U.S. policies. Many public diplomacy programs seek influence through advocacy. Our influence, like that of any professional journalistic enterprise, resides in the quality of our news reporting, current affairs shows, and features programming. Information constitutes power and influence everywhere in the world. But in societies that suppress information, as do all countries in the Middle East to one degree or another, accurate and objective news and information are especially powerful and influential.

Sawa and Alhurra: New Models within U.S. International Broadcasting

Sawa and Alhurra are examples of a new global broadcasting strategy that holds mission imperatives and market forces as co-equal in the overall broadcasting (and public diplomacy) equation. The strategy recognizes that we must marry the broadcast mission to the particular circumstances of individual markets (countries or regions) in order to cultivate an audience for our objective journalism. Because each market is different, each requires its own tailored broadcasting strategy.

The new strategy is an important evolution of U.S. international broadcasting. Long-form broadcasts via shortwave radio that worked during the Cold War are often lost in today's more sophisticated global media markets. Captive audiences in closed societies have now become savvy consumers in media-rich environments. Largely favorable attitudes toward the United States and U.S. policies have given way to widespread anti-Americanism. To reach people today, U.S. international broadcasting must demonstrate unprecedented understanding of markets and audiences and find a way to make our mission-driven programming resonate. That is precisely what Sawa and Alhurra aim to do in the Middle East.

Questions persist, nonetheless, about the need to have created Sawa and Alhurra in the first place. Some assert that the VOA Arabic service was a quality news and information product for decision makers and opinion shapers ("elites") that simply needed better distribution to attract a wider audience. Others argue that launching our own 24/7 TV channel was unnecessary and a waste of money when we could more effectively reach our desired audiences with U.S.-produced programming distributed over popular Arab TV networks.

Moving Beyond VOA's One-Size-Fits-All Radio

Radio Sawa was created as a pilot program for U.S. international broadcasting, allowing the BBG to bring to bear modern, commercial broadcasting techniques in the field of public diplomacy. It is an answer to those who asked why America, arguably the world's media leader, could not present a more viable broadcast product in the Middle East.

Well before the events of 9/11, the Board had identified the Middle East as a priority for U.S. international broadcasting. For a host of reasons, VOA Arabic was unable to attract a significant audience. It was broadcasting a one-size-fits-all, seven-hour programming stream for the entire Middle East despite substantial regional differences in language and culture. It employed no audience targeting or modern radio formats. It relied largely on shortwave and AM transmission though FM had become the dominant means of radio distribution in the region. It featured long programming blocks, instead of the shorter, faster-paced programming preferred by listeners.

Surveys in the region from 1998-2000 showed that only a very small proportion of people in the Middle East were even aware VOA Arabic existed, despite its having been on the air since 1950. Weekly listening rates among the general population across the Middle East were in the low single digits (see figure 1). Even in the one place where VOA had local FM—Kuwait—less than 2 percent tuned in weekly for Arabic broadcasting.

FIGURE I. VOA Arabic weekly listenership (percent of general population age 15+)

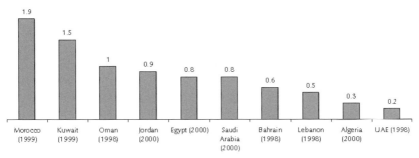

Source: Broadcasting Board of Governors data (multiple studies 1998-2000).

Hence, distribution was not the only problem.

Focus group research showed that audiences perceived VOA as biased, essentially a mouthpiece for the U.S. government. Listeners reported the service had a distant, detached feel and sound. Many said it lacked a clear, contemporary identity in an increasingly crowded media marketplace in the Middle East. An Egyptian lawyer who was an occasional listener to VOA Arabic put it this way: "The Arab listener does not feel...targeted when listening to this station, because it is an American station speaking in Arabic in the name of America."[2]

In February 2001, I led a BBG fact-finding trip to Qatar, Jordan, Egypt, the West Bank, and Israel. We met with senior Arab government officials, radio and TV broadcasters, journalists, media executives, academics and others, as well as U.S. ambassadors and embassy personnel. They all roundly affirmed what the research had already indicated: BBG needed to overhaul its broadcast product if we were to be a player in the region.

This was brought home during the trip by a U.S. government official who candidly explained that local embassy staff faced a dilemma when proposing to senior State Department officials, including the secretary of state, which media to appear on in the region. Should they recommend our own official VOA, even though it had hardly any audience, or should they

---

2. Female participant in focus group in Egypt, November 2000.

suggest one of several very popular Arab networks? The decision, we were told, was not difficult: the Arab networks got the nod every time.

Although growing anti-Americanism in the Middle East cast doubt on whether governments in the region would cooperate with us, we were met with warm receptions throughout the trip, and we uncovered opportunities for local broadcasting distribution.

Following the trip, and after consulting with the Administration and Congress, the Board redirected $3 million of BBG funding to the pilot project that would become Radio Sawa. In the aftermath of 9/11, this modest outlay was met with additional appropriations to expand and improve the new network.

Choosing the TV Network Model over TV Syndication

There is still debate within public diplomacy circles as to whether the U.S. government should pursue a syndication model rather than establish and control its own stations or networks. Proponents of syndication in the Middle East have argued for distributing U.S.-produced programming over Arab satellite channels.

Syndication can be an excellent means of distribution, but it works only when the programming content jibes with the format, philosophy, and commercial interests of the carrier.   Otherwise, it is a misfit. In the Middle East, syndication of U.S.-produced news and current affairs would be highly problematic.

First, there is the issue of access. BBG would surely want no association with government-controlled Arab media that routinely censor the news and harangue the United States. At the same time, popular independent Arab networks like al Jazeera would be very hard pressed to sacrifice their own broadcast time. Actual syndication options would likely be with third-tier networks offering limited audience reach.

Secondly, there is the issue of content. Time-sensitive news is out of the question. Even news partnerships are problematic. In the late-1990s, VOA quickly ended a joint news venture with the Middle East Broadcasting Corporation when it could not ensure editorial control over programming content. Placing politically sensitive current affairs programming is equally dubious. The only likely viable option would be some form of non-news, features programming. It remains to be seen how this might work, but the challenge is not simply to place attractive programming, but also to serve a U.S. public diplomacy mission while meeting the programming interests of the host network.

In short, syndicating U.S.-produced programming on Arab media is worth a look, but it is fraught with challenges. Even when it is an option, audience reach is episodic, waxing and waning with intermittent program placement. Also, syndicated shows are susceptible to being cancelled in times of crisis or tension, just when they are needed most. Certainly, syndication is no substitute for the U.S. government having its own TV channel, especially in the top-priority Middle East, where our national security interests require open channels of communication with Arab audiences.

Reaching Large Audiences of All Ages

Sawa and Alhurra seek to reach the largest possible audiences consistent with their mission. To do this, Sawa targets young adults, 15 to 30, while Alhurra aims to attract news-seekers of all ages. The two work in tandem to reach a cross-section of Arabs, young and old. It is important to note that such targeting does not mean Sawa does not attract older listeners or that Alhurra does not draw younger viewers. Actually, each achieves a good mix. The purpose of the targeting is to inform station positioning, branding, formatting, and programming. Each is key to broadcasting success, but none is possible to do well, or at all, absent clear audience targets.

To build large audiences for our mission-driven programming, we have to exploit the relative strengths of radio and TV as broadcast media. Modern radio is largely a medium of formats. In the U.S. context, these include news, talk, sports, and various types of music. By formatting a radio station in a specific way, we can appeal to a specific audience segment. At home, people often listen to the same radio station all day. In cars, they have preset buttons on their radios to quickly get to stations whose formats they prefer. Using an Arabic-Western popular music format is the best means of attracting large numbers of Arab youths, who then stay tuned for newscasts.

Television, in contrast, is largely a medium of programs. TV targets audience segments program by individual program. As a result, most people do not tune to a specific TV channel and leave it on all day. In the Middle East, where program guides are not readily available, "channel surfing" is especially common. Airing a wide range of appealing shows allows Alhurra to attract a much more diverse audience than would be the case if it provided 24/7 news programming. And again, with frequent newscasts and updates, people who otherwise would not watch Alhurra's news do so.

Radio and TV are mass media that, by definition, are vehicles to reach mass audiences measured in millions. Modern broadcasting, as just discussed, leverages the strengths of these media to maximize audience reach. If we seek to reach only elites, then we should consider the Internet or non-traditional vehicles such as direct mail. Similarly, public diplomacy, at its best, adds value by engaging in large-scale government-to-people communication that complements the outreach traditional diplomacy already undertakes to elites such as government officials, media owners and editors, and leading academics, among others. Too often, in my experience, when government broadcasters lay claim to an elite audience it is because they have failed to show a significant following among the general population.

In the Middle East, the elite versus mass audience discussion becomes almost moot, as 60-70 percent of the population is under age 30. Few of the region's young adults qualify as elites by any definition usually applied. Arabs aged 30 and under number 180-210 million people, many of them unemployed and disaffected. They enjoy few opportunities for social mobility and progress. They are ripe for exploitation by radical Islamic fundamentalist ideology and elements of Arab media that seek to incite them. Reaching them is key.

A further, important reason to reach mass audiences is that genuine democratic transformations are almost always mass movements. In Poland, Lech Walesa was the leader, but Solidarity was the movement. In Czechoslovakia, Vaclav Havel was the leader, but the Velvet Revolution had mass appeal. And so it went across central and eastern Europe as the Iron Curtain fell. To promote freedom and democracy during the Cold War, RFE/RL and VOA reached mass audiences. Today, U.S. international broadcasting needs to reach similarly large audiences to achieve the same effect.

Competing on an Uneven Playing Field

It is difficult to overstate the obstacles Sawa and Alhurra face as they seek to fulfill their mission and vision in the Middle East. There is hardly a broadcasting environment in the world today more difficult than that in the Middle East (see box 1). The range of challenges, encompassing both political and media factors, is daunting. They include fierce anti-Americanism, hostility toward U.S. government media presence in the region, rising media competition overall, government resistance, and inherent difficulties in reaching youths with news and information.

Recent opinion surveys in the Middle East point to rising Anti-Americanism. Hostility toward the United States complicates the work of Sawa and Alhurra in two important ways. First, there is a potential turn-off factor that might keep some people from tuning in at all. Second, when they do tune in, their anti-Americanism naturally makes them more skeptical, even cynical, about the news and information we broadcast.

The main drivers of the anti-Americanism are opposition to U.S. policy on Israeli-Palestinian affairs and U.S. involvement in Iraq. Reports on each fill the newscasts of Arab radio and TV and the front pages of

---

Box 1. The Middle Eastern Media Environment

None of the sixteen Arab states of the Middle East and North Africa is a democracy. In this context, free expression by the media is limited and self-censorship is common. Government agencies control media directly or have the power to grant or deny licenses to TV and radio stations. However, with the emergence of satellite TV—and the Internet to a lesser extent—governments are losing their information monopoly. To compete with popular satellite channels such as al Jazeera and al Arabiya, many countries have established state-funded satellite channels, but few attract large audiences.

State-run TV and FM radio stations dominate the media market but have faced increasing competition over the last decade. Governments typically limit the number of private FM broadcasters and domestic TV channels available: Bahrain, Libya, Oman, Tunisia, and Yemen have no private FM broadcasters. Jordan, Kuwait, Saudi Arabia, UAE, and the West Bank have between four and eight private FM stations. Only Lebanon and Iraq have ten or more private FM stations.

Lebanon is by far the most open domestic TV market, with seventeen private TV stations. Morocco, Saudi Arabia, and the West Bank each have one private TV station. Most countries have only state-run TV stations. The real competition to state-run TV comes from satellite channels. Access to satellite TV is increasingly pervasive throughout the Middle East and parts of North Africa. As many as 90 percent of all households in the wealthier Gulf countries have access to satellite TV. In less affluent countries, such as Egypt, that figure drops to 25 percent. According to the latest estimates, there are about 73 million potential adult satellite TV viewers from Morocco to Oman.

In most countries—specifically, Bahrain, Egypt, Jordan, Kuwait, Lebanon, Oman, Qatar, Saudi Arabia, Syria, UAE, and Yemen—viewers have access to between 15 and 180 satellite TV channels, depending on location and financial resources. Viewers who can receive both NileSat and ArabSat satellite networks can watch about 125 channels for free, and 262 if they pay for additional subscriber-only channels.

Rather than using TV listings, viewers in the Middle East and North Africa tend to constantly channel-surf, making competition among TV channels even more intense.

---

newspapers every day. Constant media content that portrays the United States as the enemy of the Arab people hardly helps promote other U.S. government activities like Sawa and Alhurra.

Much of the Arab print media has not wanted the Arab people to have a chance to make up their own minds about our new broadcasting initiatives, particularly Alhurra. Newspaper articles attacked Alhurra before the channel even went on the air. Commentary from *al Khaleej* newspaper in the United Arab Emirates as typical: "This media offensive does not differ from the military, political and economic invasion as well as the terror (of the United States) . . . The only way to improve the American image is to change policy in the region and let the people choose their fate freely."

Negative Arab press coverage may have biased some potential Alhurra viewers, but the larger challenge over the long run is the growing diversity and sophistication of media, both Arab and foreign, in the Middle East. Gaining and keeping audience is every media outlet's daily preoccupation, and Sawa and Alhurra are no different. While Sawa's unique format and programming mix know no rivals in the region, in places like Jordan and Egypt copy-cat stations have emerged. Alhurra, on the other hand, is in a fiercely competitive satellite TV arena, which will only grow in intensity.

In addition to competition from other media, Sawa faces uncooperative governments in selected countries. Sawa is an FM network, yet Saudi Arabia and Egypt have not yet made FM licenses available, despite repeated BBG requests. Cross-border AM is the back-up distribution means, but it is neither the preferred mode of radio listening nor ideal for Sawa's format.

While Sawa reaches large numbers of youths, the youth market will only bear so much news. Reaching them with information requires great skill and creativity. Our research shows that Arab youths prefer short but frequent news updates on the radio. That is why Sawa broadcasts news twice an hour 24/7.

Much has been made of Sawa and Alhurra's "media war" with Arab networks. We are not in a media war with al Jazeera, al Arabiya, or any other Arab network. We are keeping our eye on the ball—promoting freedom and democracy—using objective journalism as our tool.

Al Jazeera and al Arabiya transcend traditional media roles. They function, in effect, as quasi-political movements, reflecting two of the defining characteristics of the Middle East today. One is the lack of political and press freedom. The other is Arab nationalism. Arab networks manifest both. They cover the news Arab regimes suppress, and they cover the news that implicitly reinforces the fiercely nationalist perspective of many Arabs. There is constant coverage on al Jazeera, al Arabiya, and other Arab networks of the Israeli-Palestinian conflict and the U.S. intervention in Iraq. They are eminently newsworthy topics and, at the same time, topics that intensely arouse Arab passions.

Needless to say, it is neither Sawa nor Alhurra's mission to become the voice of the Arab people in their grievances against Israel and the United States. We are also not expecting to take al Jazeera or al Arabiya's audience.

We are happy to share audiences that naturally turn to indigenous news sources, often first.

Marrying the Mission to the Market in the Middle East

In the face of enormous political antagonism and media challenges, how do Sawa and Alhurra take their mandate from Congress—to promote freedom and democracy through objective journalism—and make it resonate with the largest possible audience?

To capture the attention of listeners and viewers, Sawa and Alhurra have developed unique listening and viewing propositions, respectively. That is, they each offer Arab audiences something desirable they do not already get on other radio and TV outlets in the Middle East.

Radio Sawa is designed to be a forward-looking, optimistic, empowering radio station, an example of the American spirit of openness to new ideas and cultural diversity. The station's unique blend of Western and Arabic popular music reaches out to the wide Arabic youth audience. Its up-to-the-minute comprehensive news gives listeners of all ages in the Middle East the kind of dependable radio news source not available elsewhere.

Alhurra is designed to appeal to a broad Arabic-speaking audience interested in fresh perspectives on the news and "food for thought" on a variety of subjects from health to technology to news from the world of entertainment. The station's respect for its audience and message of personal empowerment is in stark contrast to the messages of victimization put out by the major government-controlled TV channels in the region.

Neither Sawa nor Alhurra is international broadcasting in the traditional sense. Both are conceived to be local in flavor yet American in spirit. They radiate respect for the individual and the free marketplace of ideas. They reach out and connect with audiences that are overwhelmingly hostile to U.S. foreign policy but attracted to many things American—most of all, the American idea of personal freedom. By exemplifying freedom and democracy, rather than by preaching freedom and democracy, Sawa and Alhurra seek a permanent place in the Arabic-language media scene.

While strategically positioned, Sawa and Alhurra are also attractively presented. Sawa is a seamless radio product with industry-leading production values that projects an upbeat, inviting, and contemporary sound and feel. Alhurra is visually stunning television from its trademark Arabian horses to its expertly crafted station IDs to its state-of-the-art studio sets. The stations are a pleasure to listen to and watch. Manifesting the imagery of the modern Arab world, we believe they will increasingly become an integral part of the daily lives of Arabs across the Middle East.

Formatting on radio, as noted, is key to building audience. People seek predictability with radio, and a consistent format—be it news, talk, sports, music, or some other—ensures that. Sawa has a unique format among major radio stations in the Middle East, blending Western and Arabic popular music. This combination successfully draws large audiences of young Arabs. The fact that Sawa broadcasts around-the-clock rather than in short, daily transmission strengthens the appeal of the format. Audiences know what to expect with Sawa, and they can have it whenever they want it.

BOTH SAWA AND ALHURRA ARE CONCEIVED TO BE LOCAL IN FLAVOR YET AMERICAN IN SPIRIT. THEY RADIATE RESPECT FOR THE INDIVIDUAL AND THE FREE MARKETPLACE OF IDEAS. THEY REACH OUT AND CONNECT WITH AUDIENCES THAT ARE OVERWHELMINGLY HOSTILE TO U.S. FOREIGN POLICY BUT ATTRACTED TO MANY THINGS AMERICAN—MOST OF ALL, THE AMERICAN IDEA OF PERSONAL FREEDOM.

The Middle East is a complex region with major differences across countries in culture and language. So, Sawa takes its innovative approach to programming a step further. Based on the same format, Sawa broadcasts six different programming streams in recognition of the region's differences. There is a separate stream that reflects local music tastes and language dialects for Iraq, Morocco, the Gulf, Egypt, Jordan and the West Bank, and Sudan and Yemen. This regionalization of format makes Sawa, in effect, six separate radio stations.

Positioning, branding, and formatting are each important to the key tasks of attracting an audience and to fulfilling our mission. But audiences are not just drawn to media because of the way a radio station sounds or a TV station looks. They are often in search of news as well as music or entertainment. And, of course, disseminating news and information is the core BBG mission.

Sawa and Alhurra share the same news director, the same professional standards, the same regional and global network of correspondents, and the same commitment to covering the news straight. They report the news without opinion and politically charged adjectives. With flexible programming formats and correspondents worldwide, Sawa and Alhurra are able to interrupt regularly scheduled programming and mobilize to cover any story, anywhere, anytime.

Sawa has one of the largest Arabic-language radio news departments in the world, with correspondents and stringers throughout the Middle East and beyond. The station broadcasts over five hours of news each day in

325 newscasts per week. Every hour at 15 and 45 minutes past the hour, Sawa provides 5-15 minute updates. Keeping the news concise and direct specifically serves the needs and preferences of youths. Unlike the censored media in much of the Arab world, Sawa's news is accurate and objective, presenting U.S. policies in their proper context. Newscasts focus on the most important events in the region and the world, tailored specifically for the Middle East audience. Sawa programming streams share the same news content, except for the Iraq stream, which features more news overall and targets its news to Iraq.

Of Alhurra's 24-hour schedule, 14 of those hours are news and information. On Alhurra-Iraq that number rises to 17. Alhurra features two hour-long newscasts daily in primetime along with daily talk shows and roundtables to examine in depth all sides of the most important news stories of the day. The channel routinely reports on human rights abuses and political demonstrations. It also features the ongoing transition to democracy in Iraq. Alhurra, for example, was the only Arabic-language channel to broadcast the first meeting of the Iraqi National Congress in its entirety. Showing examples of democracy in action constitutes poignant programming in a region of non-democratic governments.

While Sawa and Alhurra provide audiences with up-to-date news and information, to meet the preferences of Arab audiences, both stations also air a wide range of current affairs programs, editorial comment, lifestyle shows, and hourly interactive features. These are designed to broaden our audiences' view of the world and foster political expression.

Sawa, for example, broadcasts numerous regular features that support the freedom and democracy mission and encourage audiences to expand their world. These include:

- **The Free Zone:** Sawa's signature program on freedom and democracy issues in the Middle East, including interviews with democracy advocates throughout the region on human rights, freedom of the press, elections, women's rights, and related topics.
- **Ask The World Now:** An innovative presentation of U.S. policies and editorial comment that uses statements from senior U.S. policymakers.
- **SawaChat:** Sawa's flagship interactive feature, broadcast hourly, providing the audience an opportunity to express opinions on political and social issues of interest to Arab youths in response to the question of the day.
- **What's New:** An upbeat feature program focusing on

happenings in literature, the Internet, DVDs, cinema, music, science, and technology. Presenting Arab and Western culture in the same context, the program promotes openness to new ideas and acceptance of regional and national differences.

- **You and Your Health:** Authoritative information about personal health and fitness.

Like Sawa, Alhurra complements its daily newscasts and newsbriefs with a host of current affairs discussion programs as well as lifestyle features that not only inform but also expand audience awareness of the world around them. These include:

- **Free Hour:** A one-hour daily talk show, examining the latest news and issues with expert analysis and debate.
- **Alhurra Presents:** An hour-long weekly conversation with a prominent newsmaker.
- **All Directions:** Weekly talk show with newsmakers and experts on topical issues in the Middle East.
- **Free Debate:** Weekly one-hour talk show that tackles social issues in the region, including family issues such as spousal abuse.
- **Talk of Two Rivers:** Weekly talk show that provides in-depth analysis of the previous week's events in Iraq.
- **Alhurra Sports Weekly:** A focus on Middle Eastern sports.
- **Cinemagazine:** Profiles a different movie each week, with actor interviews and background footage.
- **I-Tech:** Brings the latest in computer and information technology to the Middle East.
- **The New Explorers:** Documents the most important scientific work of our time.

Obviously, the best programming is for naught if it cannot be heard or seen. It was the BBG's success in acquiring FM broadcast licenses in key

---

Recognizing that Arab and Muslim audiences rely on satellite television and radio, the government has begun some promising initiatives in television and radio broadcasting to the Arab world, Iran, and Afghanistan. These efforts are beginning to reach large audiences. The Broadcasting Board of Governors has asked for much larger resources. It should get them.
                                                    —The 9/11 Commission Report

Middle Eastern cities that launched Sawa as a viable local broadcaster, and the surety of being accessible on ArabSat and NileSat that put Alhurra in the satellite TV game. To be sure, there are ample virgin broadcast areas in which to establish new FM stations. Sawa's distribution remains very much in a growth mode.

Initial Success: Key Research Findings

Performance measurement in any enterprise takes place relative to the mission. Our mission is to promote freedom and democracy through objective journalism, so we want to know, whom are we reaching, and do our audiences trust what we air, specifically the news?

Weekly audience is a measure of those who listen at least once per week. By capturing information this way, we learn regularity of use, an important nuance, for it implies commitment on the part of the listener or viewer. Weekly listening or viewing measured repeatedly is thus more than just a simple snapshot in time of how many people happened to be tuned in. We are pleased that both Sawa listening rates and Alhurra viewing rates show extraordinary audience acceptance thus far.

News reliability measures listeners' and viewers' assessment of the news component of the programming. This information is extremely useful as an indicator that people listening to attractive music or features do not simply tune out when the news comes on the American stations. As data presentations in the next section will show, news on both Sawa and Alhurra score high for reliability among audience members.

Sawa and Alhurra are products of intensive market and audience research unprecedented in U.S. international broadcasting. Knowing how to position, brand, program, and distribute them has required in-depth understanding of the media environments and the target audiences. Programming concepts and prototypes are routinely vetted in focus groups. Exploration of how best to cover sensitive content issues is carried out through in-depth, one-on-one interviews. Musical preferences are surveyed weekly in selected cities across the region. The aim is to ensure an overall approach and specific content that meets audience needs while fulfilling the BBG mission.

We use research not only to drive Sawa and Alhurra performance but also to measure it. Twice yearly, independent surveys by ACNielsen sweep across a group of Middle Eastern countries, focusing on places where Sawa has local distribution. These surveys have given us a clear sense of how Sawa and Alhurra are doing according to the measures just discussed.

We are very encouraged by what we see. Both Sawa and Alhurra are still young. Because of the media and political challenges they face, we never expected them to become market leaders overnight. In fact, we never expected them to have the market acceptance they have already won. The targets we set for official government measurement were ambitious by the standards of government-supported international broadcasting—at 5 percent weekly audience for Sawa and 10 percent for Alhurra— and we have far exceeded those almost everywhere.

The following charts tell a compelling story.[3] They speak to some of the frequent questions surrounding Sawa and Alhurra since their inception: Would Arabs even bother to tune in U.S. government-supported stations? Would Arabs, feeling the hostility they do toward America, trust the stations, especially for news? Would Sawa attract Arab youths but fail to draw older, presumably more mature, adults? Would Sawa draw a mass audience at the expense of an "elite" audience? We now have answers to these questions, and they are uniformly positive.

Sawa does exceedingly well in attracting broad audiences of all ages wherever it has local FM distribution (FM being the best method of transmission to reach a young audience), as shown in figure 2. In those local markets, Sawa is consistently among the most popular radio stations. In Egypt and Saudi Arabia, Sawa is available only on cross-border AM (approval of BBG requests for FM licenses is still pending in both countries). As a reference point, among weekly listening rates for all U.S. international broadcasting language services, the median is roughly 6 percent.

Within its target audience of 15-29 year-olds, Sawa does even better (figure 3). Morocco and Qatar listening rates, in the mid- to high-70 percent range, are among the very highest rates ever recorded for U.S. international broadcasting services. I would reiterate the strategic importance of this demographic, constituting 60-70 percent of populations across the Middle East and being a prime age for recruitment into radical political/religious movements.

---

3. Research findings presented here for Sawa and Alhurra are based on surveys conducted by ACNielsen in Egypt, UAE, Kuwait, Jordan, Morocco, and Saudi Arabia in August 2004 and a national survey of Iraq conducted by a separate research group also in July-August 2004. Findings for Sawa from an ACNielsen survey in Qatar in March 2004 are also included. Face-to-face interviews were conducted in Arabic with the following sample sizes: Egypt (2,007), UAE (1,202 in Abu Dhabi and Dubai only), Kuwait (1,501), Jordan (1,500), Morocco (1,325 in the seven cities where Radio Sawa is on FM), Saudi Arabia (2,001), Qatar (1000 in Doha only), and Iraq (2,500). Surveys included 50 percent men and 50 percent women representative of key demographic groups in terms of social class, education, employment, size and type of household. Margin of error: +/- 2.6 percent. The results from urban surveys cannot be projected to the national populations of these countries as they were conducted in major cities and were not intended to be national in scope. The urban centers sampled would constitute 20 percent to 30 percent of the home populations.

FIGURE 2. Radio Sawa weekly listenership (percent of general population age 15+)

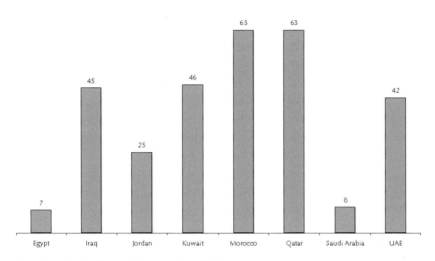

Source: Broadcasting Board of Governors data, 2004.
Note: The standard measurement for government-supported international broadcasting is weekly, meaning listening at least once during the seven days prior to the survey, per the industry standards set by the Conference of International Broadcasting Audience Research, London.

FIGURE 3. Radio Sawa weekly listenership (percent of general population 15-29)

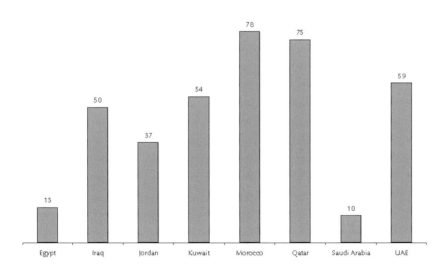

Source: Broadcasting Board of Governors data, 2004.

Listening to Sawa among elites is also high, confirming that attracting a mass audience does not preclude reaching elites as well (figure 4). This is a significant finding in light of the public diplomacy debate over elite vs. mass audiences. Sawa shows that gaining both is possible.

It is essential to Sawa's success that it not only reach large audiences but that those audiences trust the news it broadcasts. Findings on Sawa's reliability, illustrated in figure 5, confirm that Sawa is a trusted source. That such high rates of news reliability would emerge among populations that are uniformly anti-American is remarkable and attests to the professionalism of Sawa's news programming.

The BBG has been conducting quantitative studies of Sawa since shortly after the station's debut two and a half years ago. The findings presented are broadly consistent with what we have seen all along. Sawa's staying power, its ability not only to attract but also to retain large audiences that trust its news, is further evidence of its success.

Alhurra, in contrast, had only been on the air six months by the time of the surveys in August 2004. A limited telephone survey in April 2004 had provided a glimpse of its early reach, but now we have more robust data to make a more complete assessment (figure 6).

FIGURE 4. Radio Sawa weekly listenership (percent of "elites," social classes A&B)

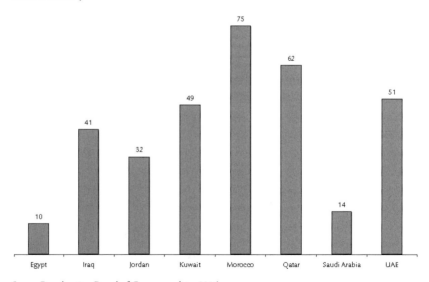

Source: Broadcasting Board of Governors data, 2004.
Note: Social classes A&B refer to society's well-educated managers and professionals per the industry-standard A-E classification of the European Society for Opinion and Marketing Research.

FIGURE 5. Percentage of weekly listeners answering the question, "How reliable is the news and information one can hear on Radio Sawa?" with "very or somewhat reliable"

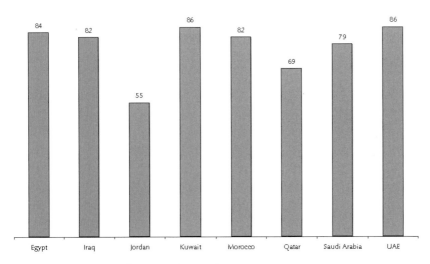

Source: Broadcasting Board of Governors data, 2004.

FIGURE 6. Alhurra TV weekly viewership (percentage of general population age 15+ in households with satellite reception)

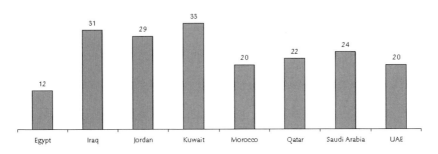

Source: Broadcasting Board of Governors data, 2004.

These levels of viewing for Alhurra indicate that the station has begun to establish an audience at levels that are very good for a new market entrant in a crowded media environment. Especially given the anti-Americanism in the region and the negative comments in the Arab press about Alhurra, this early success is encouraging.

The news reliability data for Alhurra are also encouraging, for the same reason cited above for Sawa (see figure 7). It seems reasonable to assume that record Arab hostility toward the U.S. would all but rule out any U.S. government-sponsored media outlet being seen as trustworthy. That this has not proved true augurs well for Alhurra's prospects to build a larger audience over time.

FIGURE 7.   **Percentage of weekly Alhurra TV viewers answering the question, "Do you think the news on Alhurra is very reliable, somewhat reliable, neither reliable nor unreliable, somewhat unreliable, or very unreliable?" with "very reliable" or "somewhat reliable"**

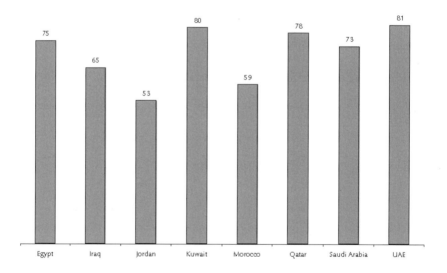

Source: Broadcasting Board of Governors data, 2004.

In sum, research shows that Sawa and Alhurra have achieved excellent results so far. Where it has FM delivery, Sawa is often the number one station in its individual markets, not only among international stations but also among all stations. In a field dominated by al Jazeera and al Arabiya, Alhurra has particularly stiff competition arrayed against it. But for a recently created foreign station, it has done quite well. Both stations achieve very good news reliability scores, even in the pervasive anti-American atmosphere into which they broadcast. In addition, recent qualitative research has shown the appeal of non-hard news programming that provides important social, cultural, and economic content. We have every expectation that both stations will get even stronger, and that Alhurra will gradually build its audience.

Building on Success

Odds are, had anyone proposed three years ago that today we could have some 24 million Arab adults tuned in weekly to U.S.-supported radio and TV services, he would have been lampooned. But that is exactly what we now have. Opening new channels of mass communication with the people of the Middle East is a vital contribution to overall U.S. foreign policy goals in the region.

As we build on Sawa and Alhurra's success, we need to bear in mind what they are aiming to do. They seek to promote freedom and democracy over the long run through objective journalism. In doing this, they not only present the news but also present a forward-looking vision for Arabs of all ages, one based on hope and opportunity for a better life. Critical to Sawa and Alhurra's success is to attracting and retaining large audiences who trust the stations' news and information.

Only by playing it straight with skeptical Arab audiences can we hope to have the necessary credibility to ensure success. The Board and the managers of Sawa and Alhurra must do whatever is necessary to safeguard the stations' editorial integrity. For, if we lost our credibility, we would lose any ability to exercise the power and influence of broadcast operations that manifest the best of a free press in the American tradition.

7. America and the Arab Media Environment

Marc Lynch

On February 14, 2004, the United States launched the Arabic language satellite television station Alhurra.[1] Presented as the flagship of the Bush Administration's public diplomacy strategy for the Middle East, Alhurra—along with Radio Sawa, launched in 2002—aimed to give America a voice to balance out what was considered to be a hateful, hostile, but increasingly influential Arab media environment. To this point Alhurra has had scant success; it has little market share and no observable impact on Arab public attitudes. Part of its failure lies in the shortcomings of its content and presentation. A large part comes from the inherent lack of credibility of an American government–sponsored media outlet. But in this chapter, I will argue that the larger problem is structural, and involves basic misconceptions about the nature of the Arab media and about what a television station can plausibly achieve.

The American approach to the Arab media has been profoundly self-defeating, and it appears to rest on fundamental misunderstandings of the Arab media's nature, content, and political role. The media component of an effective public diplomacy in the region would emphasize private, free media with open and wide-ranging political coverage—and should demonstrate by example the American commitment to political freedoms.

The Arab Media Environment

The Arab media have gone through a number of clear phases of development.[2] In the 1950s and 1960s, radio broadcasting emerged as a major factor in regional politics. The Voice of the Arabs preached a pan-

---

1. It is unclear why the Broadcasting Board of Governors prefers to render the station's name as Alhurra, which violates normal Arabic transliteraton practice. The standard rendition would be al Hurra.

2. See William Rugh, *Arab Mass Media: Newspapers, Radio, and Television in Arab Politics* (Westport, CT: Greenwood, 2004) for a comprehensive overview.

Arabist message to a vast Arab audience, serving as a potent weapon in the hands of Egyptian President Gamal Abd al Nasser. In response, virtually every Arab state established its own radio station, creating a crowded environment of state-run, politically focused radio. The Arab defeat in the 1967 war with Israel, as well as the hallucinatory news broadcasts by Ahmed Said and Voice of the Arabs, destroyed its credibility, an occurrence which many observers believe—or at least hope—is repeating itself with al Jazeera after its coverage of the war in Iraq.

In the 1970s, the Arab media fell into a pall of tightly controlled state broadcasting. With an end to the radio wars of the Arab cold war, the dominant media became television, which proved far easier for states to control. The Arab press suffered from the increasing repressiveness of Arab states, which proved ever more intent on stifling and shaping all political debate. The Lebanese civil war drove much of that country's lively press into exile, establishing London as the crucial base for Arab print journalism. During this decade, Saudi Arabia used its vast oil wealth to establish control over much of the remaining independent mass media. Overall, through the 1980s a suffocating conformity stifled the Arab media and wider public sphere.

During the early 1990s, a number of Arab countries embarked on experiments in liberalization. While this did not lead to any genuine democratic transitions, it did offer a temporary *glasnost* in many Arab states. In countries such as Jordan and Yemen, the early 1990s saw the emergence of a lively, independent, critical press, although electronic media remained tightly controlled by governments. Saudi-owned transnational newspapers based in London such as *al Hayat* and *al Sharq al Awsat* appealed to elites, while *al Quds al Arabi* offered a rare critical voice free of Saudi control. Finally, in response to the eye-opening success of CNN in covering the 1990-91 Gulf crisis, a number of Arab states and investors moved to create Arab satellite television stations.[3] These stations emphasized entertainment rather than politics, however, and remained for the most part under Saudi tutelage. Even the BBC joint venture with the Saudi-owned station Orbit ended abruptly after it ran a documentary deemed offensive by the Saudi authorities.

It was not simply the technology of satellite media that revolutionized Arab politics. It was al Jazeera's independence from Saudi Arabia and its decision to emphasize politics—and especially its focus on open, contentious, public political debate—that shaped a radically new Arab media environment. Established by the emirate of Qatar after a palace coup brought the young Shaykh Hamad bin Khalifa al Thani to power, al Jazeera drew on the BBC

---

3. Naomi Sakr, *Satellite Realms: Transnational Television, Globalization and the Middle East* (New York: St. Martin's Press, 2001).

employees who had been thrown out of work by the collapse of the BBC-Orbit collaboration. It quickly established itself as something new in Arab politics with its frank and fearless coverage of sensitive political topics, as well as the unrestrained nature of its live talk shows.

Market surveys confirm the widespread belief that al Jazeera quickly established a position of unprecedented dominance in the late 1990s. In Jordan, for example, al Jazeera's audience among those who owned a satellite dish jumped from 18.9 percent in 1998 to 42 percent in 2000, while in the same period those viewing it as the most credible source for international news jumped from 24 percent to 49 percent.[4] Palestinian surveys show similar findings: by September 1999, 51 percent of Palestinians named al Jazeera as the most watched satellite television station; 47 percent said the same in February 2000.[5]

In response, other actors besides the United States moved to create competitors: importantly, al Arabiya, but also Abu Dhabi TV, LBC-al Hayat, Hizbollah's al Manar, Egypt's Dream, Saudi Arabia's al Ikhbariya, and others. The result was greater market fragmentation and intense competition. A June 2004 survey by Zogby International found that despite this competition, al Jazeera remained the most watched Arab news source overall, with some regional and local variations: it ranked as the primary station for 62 percent of Jordanians, 54 percent of Moroccans, 44 percent of Lebanese, 44 percent of Saudis, and 46 percent in the United Arab Emirates; and the secondary station for (on average) about 20 percent more in each country. Al Arabiya was next, averaging about 7-8 percent in most (but 19 percent in the UAE), while LBC did well only in Lebanon (29 percent), and Abu Dhabi TV did well in Saudi Arabia (22 percent) and the UAE (17 percent). In contrast to widely cited surveys commissioned by the Broadcasting Board of Governors (BBG), in independent studies Alhurra barely appeared.[6] In June 2004, for example, a survey by the Palestinian Center for Policy and Survey Research found that 58.1 percent of Palestinians most watched al Jazeera, compared with 10.2 percent watching al Arabiya, 12 percent al Manar, and only 1.1 percent Alhurra.[7] An April

---

4. "Democracy in Jordan" annual surveys conducted by the Center for Strategic Studies at the University of Jordan, http://www.css-jordan.org/polls/democracy/2003/index.html.

5. Palestinian Center for Policy and Survey Research, Public Opinion Poll #43, September 1999, and Public Opinion Poll #47, February 2000.

6. The Alhurra survey was reported by Reuters; "Arabs are Watching U.S. TV Channel Alhurra," April 29, 2004. Zogby International poll conducted for Shibley Telhami, May–June 2004.

7. Palestinian Center for Policy and Survey Research, Public Opinion Poll #12, June 2004, http://www.pcpsr.org/survey/polls/2004/p12b.html.

2004 Gallup poll found that, even in Iraq under American occupation, only 6 percent of Iraqis had viewed Alhurra in the last seven days.[8] A survey in Saudi Arabia by the Arab Advisors Group found that only 16 percent of Saudis regularly watched Alhurra, compared with 82 percent regularly viewing al Jazeera and 75 percent watching al Arabiya.[9]

Of the challengers to al Jazeera's Arab market share, perhaps the most intriguing and most successful has been the Dubai-based al Arabiya. In February 2003, with $300 million in start-up money from Saudi Arabia, technologically advanced facilities taken over from MBC, and a veteran team of broadcasters, al Arabiya set out to offer a more moderate (and, of course, more deferential to Saudi sensitivities) alternative to al Jazeera. However, al Arabiya emphasized professionalism, objectivity, and "moderate" politics over freedom or pushing the boundaries of public discourse. As its Jordanian managing director Salah al Qallab revealingly stated, "We are not going to make problems for Arab countries."[10] During the Iraq war, as it struggled to establish itself, al Arabiya imitated al Jazeera and won some success, especially among Iraqis, Saudis, and Kuwaitis who distrusted al Jazeera's alleged sympathies with Saddam's regime. After the war, Saudi Arabia reigned in al Arabiya, and appointed the pro-American former editor of *al Sharq al Awsat*, Abd al Rahman al Rashed, as its managing director. Like Alhurra, al Arabiya self-consciously set out to avoid using terms such as "martyrdom" or "resistance," instead adopting the "neutral" vocabulary preferred by American critics of the Arab media. Compared with al Jazeera, al Arabiya played down the Palestine issue while devoting a lot of time to covering Iraq, employing a more positive spin in line with American preferences. It ran into problems, even so: several of its correspondents were killed or arrested; the Iraqi Governing Council shut down its operations several times, just as it did al Jazeera's; and on October 30, its offices in Baghdad were decimated by a massive car bomb. Al Arabiya talk shows tended to feature more Saudi and other Arab officials— foreign ministers, members of Parliament—and fewer independent and critical personalities than did the al Jazeera programs. Arab officials who feared al Jazeera made time for al Arabiya to promote it as a safer version of satellite media. It was not an accident that when President George W. Bush chose to grant interviews to the Arab media to contain the damage of the Abu Ghraib scandal, he chose al Arabiya (along with the American station, Alhurra) as the outlet. However, it is important to note how the

---

8. *Arab News*, September 10, 2004.

9. CNN/USA Today/Gallup Poll, http://i.a.cnn.net/cnn/2004/WORLD/meast/04/28/iraq.poll/iraq.poll.4.28.pdf.

10. Ian Urbina, "The Other Air War Over Iraq," *Asia Times*, March 1, 2003.

pressures of market competition shaped al Arabiya's programming, despite these intentions. Over the summer of 2004, al Arabiya broadcast numerous hostage and beheading videos, just like al Jazeera. As Rashed explained, "There is only one condition for me to stop airing all these videotapes, which is that all TV stations in the region agree not to show them."[11]

Some Arab television stations are more genuinely hostile to the United States. Moving in the other direction, al Manar Television offered a vision of Arab television as a fairly explicit propaganda machine. Run by Hizbollah in Lebanon, al Manar relied on a steady diet of provocative, horrifying images layered in an impenetrable, univocal discourse of anti-American, anti-Israeli rhetoric. Al Manar made no pretence either to objectivity or towards open dialogue, in sharp contrast to al Jazeera, which prided itself on both. While al Manar showed surprising strength in some recent Palestinian, Jordanian, and Iraqi media surveys, few have any illusions about its purpose or its missions.

This, then, is the media environment into which Alhurra arrived. Arab satellite stations compete fiercely for market share by emphasizing issues likely to reach wide Arab and Muslim audiences. Satellite dishes— legal or otherwise—have become ubiquitous. This has quickly acclimated Arab audiences to the expectation of choice and disagreement—long repressed by Arab dictatorships determined to maintain a voice monopoly. While there are certain programs that command loyal audiences, such as Faisal al Qassem's *The Opposite Direction*, or the Lebanese reality show *Superstar*, for news Arab viewers tend to switch rapidly from station to station. Well-versed in the arts of deciphering political codes in the authoritarian media, these audiences now excel in comparing coverage and analysis, and triangulating. Growing numbers of Arab elites have direct access to American broadcasting and the Internet. CNN, the BBC, and even Fox News are available via satellite, and Arabs routinely surf among these stations even as they prefer al Jazeera as their primary source of information. Indeed, the overly nationalistic and controlled nature of American coverage of the invasion of Iraq contributed to the popularity of al Jazeera and other Arab stations; rather than a choice between objective news and al Jazeera, many Arabs saw the American media as equally biased in support of American policies, a view that has been reinforced by the steady drumbeat of revelations since the war about the absence of weapons of mass destruction and the failure of the American media to challenge the Bush Administration's dubious claims.

---

11. As quoted in Associated Press, "Arab TV Stations Debate Use of Videos Supplied by Camera-Toting Militants," August 16, 2004.

American officials have, unfortunately, frequently misunderstood this Arab media environment. In a February 2003 explanation of the need for Alhurra, Kenneth Tomlinson, chair of the BBG, told the Senate that "had Secretary Powell delivered that speech [to the UN] only two years ago… most people in the Arab Middle East would have heard it only through the distorting filter of radio and television stations controlled by those hostile to the United States."[12] This is untrue. Arab audiences would have seen the speech delivered live on al Jazeera and other Arab media, which regularly broadcast a surprising number of American press conferences, speeches, and other policy statements. The amount of such content has increased in recent years as the direct American presence in the region has grown. When President Bush gave one of his rare press conferences in May 2004 to defend his Iraq policy, for example, al Jazeera broadcast it live and unedited, while Alhurra did not. Similarly, both al Jazeera and al Arabiya carried live coverage of Rumsfeld's Senate testimony about the Abu Ghraib prison scandal.

In April 2004, Mouafac Harb, news director for Radio Sawa and Alhurra, told the Senate that "Arab independent media is a myth" because all the media were owned by governments or by ruling families. How Alhurra, owned and operated by the American government, would challenge that phenomenon was unclear. Nor did this accurately convey the essential difference between al Jazeera and traditional state-run television stations. Harb further claimed that "in the past few years, the Middle East has been a two-channel television market [with] the ratings for these two channels largely determined by one person and not [by] good journalism, and that person is Osama bin Laden."[13] Harb argued that "people in the Arabic-speaking world got a steady diet of variations of just one story, Arab humiliation," a story which Alhurra would challenge. In the next section, I hope to demonstrate the extent to which this picture distorts the substance of the political debate on al Jazeera and in the Arab media.

Talk Shows

In February 2004, Thomas Friedman articulated an emerging conventional wisdom: "The U.S. ouster of Saddam Hussein has also triggered the first real 'conversation' about political reform in the Arab world in a long, long time. It is still mostly in private, but more is now erupting in public."[14]

---

12. Senate Committee on Foreign Relations, *American Public Diplomacy and Islam.* Testimony of Kenneth Y. Tomlinson. 108th congress, 1st session, February 27, 2003.

13. Senate Committee on Foreign Relations, *The Broadcasting Board of Governors: Finding the Right Media for the Message in the Middle East.* Testimony of Mouafac Harb. 108th congress, 2nd session, April 29, 2004.

14. Thomas Friedman, "Look Who's Talking," *New York Times*, February 19, 2004.

But even a cursory look at al Jazeera talk shows over the last half decade demonstrates that this is wrong. For my forthcoming book, I collected transcripts of 976 al Jazeera talk shows broadcast between 1998 and 2003.[15] Three issues dominate: Palestine, Iraq, and internal reform. Palestine is central to Arab conceptions of identity and interests, and the intense focus on it dramatically increased after the outbreak of the Palestinian uprising in September 2000. The intense, live coverage of the conflict in the Arab media galvanized Arab publics, contributing to widespread anger and fueling remarkable levels of political protest. Palestinian issues went from 24.6 percent of the talk show programming in 1999 to over a third of all programming in 2001 and 2002.

> MANY ARABS SAW THE AMERICAN MEDIA AS EQUALLY BIASED IN SUPPORT OF AMERICAN POLICIES, A VIEW THAT HAS BEEN REINFORCED BY THE STEADY DRUMBEAT OF REVELATIONS SINCE THE WAR ABOUT THE ABSENCE OF WEAPONS OF MASS DESTRUCTION AND THE FAILURE OF THE AMERICAN MEDIA TO CHALLENGE THE BUSH ADMIN-ISTRATION'S DUBIOUS CLAIMS.

From 1999–2001, Iraq was a distant second, but it clearly stood above any other conflict or single issue. In 2002–2003, it shot to the top of the list of Arab issues of conversation (44 percent of all talk shows in 2003), and the coverage of the war and its aftermath had a similar galvanizing effect on Arab audiences. In contrast to discussions of the Israeli-Palestinian conflict, however, programs on Iraq featured a vastly wider range of opinion and argument. Members of the former Iraqi opposition, Kuwaitis, and other opponents of Saddam were well-represented on al Jazeera and in other Arab media, even if their positions proved highly unpopular with public opinion.

The third primary axis of argument in these talk shows has always been the question of reform, encompassing virtually all aspects of political, social, cultural, and economic life. Almost every election in the Arab or Muslim worlds received considerable attention (although during 2003, with the heavy focus on Iraq, more elections went un-discussed), as did noticeably increased repression or protests in Arab states. Beyond specific elections, the talk shows routinely posed broad questions about "democracy and the Arab world," "the Islamist movement and democracy" (July 28, 2001, *Open Dialogue*), and "the accountability of rulers" (July 3, 2001, *The Opposite Direction*), before and after the American invasion of Iraq. If anything,

---

15. Marc Lynch, *Iraq and the New Arab Public Sphere* (New York: Columbia University Press, forthcoming).

over the last year or so the tone of the al Jazeera arguments seems to have grown coarser, angrier, and more confrontational, reflecting wider patterns of frustration and anger in Arab public opinion, while the overwhelming focus on Iraq and the United States has driven out some of the focus on internal reform.

In testimony to the Senate Foreign Relations Committee in early 2004, BBG Chairman Kenneth Tomlinson posited that "the concept of debate shows has reached the Arab world today, but parameters and the topics allowed to be discussed on these debate shows, this is what we're trying to expand."[16] This is clearly wrong. Talk shows routinely took on the most basic foundations of the Arab status quo, challenging audiences to question even the most sensitive red lines. For example, the March 5, 1999, television news show *The Opposite Direction* asked whether this generation of Arabs might succeed at democracy where their fathers failed. An August 31, 1999, *The Opposite Direction* asked how the perennial states of emergency in the Arab states could possibly be justified, while a November 2, 1999, *The Opposite Direction* explored "military regimes and their impact on society." A June 27, 2000, *The Opposite Direction* asked about the commitments of the "new Arab wealthy." A July 19, 2000, episode of *No Limits* asked about women's rights in the Arab world. A January 1, 2001, *The Opposite Direction* asked whether the Palestinian Intifada was "a waste of time." A March 27, 2001, *The Opposite Direction* looked critically at the Taliban's destruction of the great Buddha statues. A June 11, 2002, *The Opposite Direction* mocked the 99.99 percent electoral victories of Arab presidents. A July 11, 2002, *Minbar al Jazeera* took on the spread of AIDS in the Arab world. The controversial *Arab Human Development Report* released in August 2002 was discussed on several different talk shows. An April 2004 episode of *The Opposite Direction* focused attention on torture in Arab prisons. And, most cruelly, a March 7, 2003, *The Opposite Direction* asked, "Why have Arabs become the joke of the world?"

Tomlinson specifically claimed that "they are not venturing yet to talk about unemployment, education in the Middle East." Not so. The May 12, 1999, episode of *No Limits* discussed "The Arab Economic Situation," while the July 14, 1999, *No Limits* focused on "Arab workers"; the December 8, 1999, *No Limits* focused on "Arab unemployment"; the May 2, 2001, *No Limits* discussed "obstacles to investment in the Arab world"; the August 8, 2001, *No Limits* discussed "the reasons for the Arab brain drain to the

---

16. Senate Committee on Foreign Relations, *The Broadcasting Board of Governors: Finding the Right Media for the Message in the Middle East.* Testimony of Kenneth Y. Tomlinson. 108th congress, 2nd session. April 29, 2004.

West"; the February 21, 2001, *No Limits* program dealt with "the crisis of education." Perhaps Alhurra inspired the May 17, 2000, *No Limits* discussion of "the problems of Arab youth"? Without belaboring the point, the evidence does not support Tomlinson's claims.

Nor has Alhurra done better. With only five talk shows on its weekly schedule, and with what one writer described as a "deadening sameness of Arab guests," Alhurra's talk shows suggest a step backward, rather than progress.[17] While some roundtables have posed important topics, the pool of guests draws heavily on Lebanese writers, Kuwaitis, Iraqis (especially former Iraqi opposition figures), and some Egyptians. The pro-American reputations of the vast majority of the guests certainly should not disqualify them from participating, but does tend to reinforce skepticism about the station.[18] For example, a special report on the prison abuse photos in mid-May offered commentary from an American member of Congress, an American military official, the Iraqi Governing Council's National Security Advisor (a former member of the Iraqi opposition), and a former advisor to the Kuwaiti Minister of Information—not a lineup likely to reassure Arab viewers. The restrained and cautious tones of the talk shows on Alhurra (and al Arabiya), plus the fact that they are pre-recorded rather than broadcast live, suggest that in terms of free and open political debate, the American alternative to al Jazeera is less, rather than more.

The American Approach to the Arab Media

Unfortunately, the Bush Administration has approached this complex, new Arab public sphere from a simplistic conception of friends and enemies. The United States increasingly saw the new Arab media as a principle enemy in the region, pressuring Qatar to rein in al Jazeera and harassing its correspondents in the field.[19] In blaming the media for its problems, it concluded that the Arab media should be intimidated, pressured into moderating its coverage. For example, on July 15, 2004, Secretary of State Colin Powell told the U.S. Institute of Peace that "when a particular outlet, al Jazeera, does such a horrible job of presenting the news and when it takes every opportunity to slant the news, present it in the most outrageous

17. David Wilmsen, "Alhurra–Dialogue with the Deaf," *Transnational Broadcasting Studies Journal* 12 (Spring-Summer 2004).

18. My analysis of the Alhurra programming is based on program summaries graciously provided by Joan Mower of the BBG and Dierdre Kline of Alhurra. I would recommend that these program summaries be made available in Arabic and English on a significantly upgraded Alhurra Web site.

19. Marc Lynch, "Not the Enemy: The Arab Media and American Reform Efforts," *Arab Reform Bulletin* 2, no. 4 (April 2004), Carnegie Endowment for International Peace.

way... then we have to speak out and we have."[20] Secretary of Defense Donald Rumsfeld denounced al Jazeera's coverage of Iraq as "vicious, inaccurate and inexcusable."[21] The Administration has turned a blind eye when Arab governments have moved to crack down on their own media or have attacked al Jazeera. Not a word of objection could be heard, for example, when the Iraqi foreign minister warned al Jazeera and al Arabiya that they might be expelled from the country, or when Iraqi Prime Minister Iyad Allawi closed down the al Jazeera offices in Iraq for a month in August 2004. Nor did the Bush Administration say anything when Algeria closed al Jazeera's offices in protest over statements made by a guest on Faisal al Qassem's talk show, *The Opposite Direction*. This refusal to stand up for a free media has been devastating to American credibility as it attempts to promote reform in the region.

This hostile approach to the media is one with which Arab dictators are both familiar and comfortable. Arab governments have issued hundreds of complaints against al Jazeera and have regularly closed down the offices of satellite stations for airing offensive programs. Morocco responded to reports on the ongoing Western Sahara conflict in April 1999 by shutting down al Jazeera's operations in the country. Algeria—with its elections, mass violence, and Berber conflict—was the topic of no less than twenty shows; in July 2004, President Bouteflika finally responded to unwelcome attention by shutting down al Jazeera's Algerian offices. Jordan shut down al Jazeera after a guest talked about King Hussein's long-standing ties to the United States and made several uncomplimentary remarks about the late monarch.[22] Kuwait banned the station for a month in 1999 for a caller's comments, critical of the Emir, and closed the al Jazeera offices in November 2002 for being "not objective."[23] Israel attacked al Jazeera in June 2002 for "spreading hatred." Bahrain criticized al Jazeera in May 2002 for "insulting Bahrain and the Bahraini people." The Palestinian authority closed al Jazeera's offices in March 2001 in protest over its coverage. And in August 2004 the Iraqi authorities closed al Jazeera's offices for a month. In virtually all of these cases, open political argument and debate was defined as incitement, and harsh sanctions were imposed by regimes that viewed a free and critical media as an enemy. I would argue that the United States should take the lead in opposing such attacks on media freedoms rather than emulating them.

---

20. Reuters, "Powell Calls al Jazeera Coverage 'Horrible,'" July 15, 2004.

21. Defense Department Operational Update Briefing, April 15, 2004, transcript available at http://www.defenselink.mil/transcripts/2004/tr20040415-secdef0622.html.

22. Musa Kaylani and Walid Said, *Jordan Times,* August 12, 2002.

23. Reuters, World in Brief, *Washington Post,* November 4, 2002.

Whatever the merits of the Bush Administration's criticisms of al Jazeera, it has had some impact. Al Jazeera does seem to have toned down its coverage to some degree, and it appeared that its coverage of the Abu Ghraib prison scandal was relatively muted. In July 2004, al Jazeera issued an honor code, establishing rules and principles to guide its coverage intended mainly to deflect intense American criticism. On the other side, however, the American criticism has probably strengthened al Jazeera's position with Arab viewers and enhanced its reputation for courage and independence. U.S. criticism of al Jazeera has been widely cited in Arab discussions about American proposals for democratic reform in the region as a stark example of American hypocrisy on the subject.

Evaluating the New American-Arabic Media

The model of Alhurra closely mirrors the approach taken by authoritarian Arab governments towards al Jazeera: criticizing and pressuring the independent media while creating their own, friendlier media. That the Bush Administration's approach to the new Arab media is virtually identical to that of repressive, authoritarian Arab governments does America no credit. Underlying these policies has been a preference for controlling the media environment, using the media to deliver government messages rather than defending the industry as a vehicle for open and free critical dialogue. The early advertising efforts of Charlotte Beers have been heavily criticized, and I will not dwell on them here.[24] Where they are still relevant is in the mindset revealed, the philosophy of the role of the media in public diplomacy. Beers' Shared Values campaign sidestepped political issues, which are the most important factor shaping Arab attitudes towards the United States. And the advertising format left no room for dialogue or for engagement with Arab views. In short, this campaign epitomized a monologic conception of public diplomacy, one based in manipulation rather than in engagement. Both of the major media initiatives—Radio Sawa and Alhurra TV—share this basic philosophy.

Radio Sawa

Radio Sawa exemplifies another strand of this philosophy, what I call the "subliminal" approach: first attract the youth with pop music, and then slowly introduce political and news content so that we will begin to influence their political beliefs and ideas without their even realizing it. Introduced in 2002 in several Arab markets, and since expanded, Radio Sawa quickly

---

24. Nor will I discuss *Hi*, an inoffensive and insignificant lifestyle magazine developed by the U.S. Department of State.

gained an audience with its clear FM broadcast signal and its first-rate mix of Arabic and Western music. Its news content was originally minimal, with short news briefs and little substantive political content. While the amount of time devoted to news has been increased, the station's primary focus remains on its quite attractive, but politically irrelevant, music.

While the BBG considers Radio Sawa to be a "phenomenal success" based on its rapid gains in market share in its target Arab countries, the evidence is mixed. In the November 2004 report of the U.S. Advisory Commission on Public Diplomacy, for example, the BBG claimed an audience of 27 percent of Jordanian adults, which actually represents a steep decline from its earlier claimed audience of 30.4 percent in September 2003 and 40 percent in November 2002.[25] And market share tells only half the story. Radio Sawa benefited from the absence of market competition, with few rivals offering good music on a strong signal. Sawa has succeeded in attracting audiences, but there is little evidence that this has translated into receptivity to the news or politics. Indeed, it is striking that in precisely the countries where Sawa has done best, Jordan and Egypt, anti-American sentiment has risen the most precipitously. And there were opportunity costs, particularly with regard to the Voice of America. In July 2004, as reported by *USA Today*, nearly half the station's staff signed a petition accusing the BBG of "'killing VOA' by closing its Arabic radio service, reducing English-language broadcasting, and launching services with 'no editorial accountability and limited breaking news.'"[26] More substantive news and political programming has been neglected, VOA staff complained, in favor of Sawa's pop music and news bites. Finally, as former VOA deputy director Alan Heil pointed out in the same article, "'Sawa has been on the air for 26 months and has never had an independent review' of its news content for accuracy and depth."[27]

Alhurra TV

Unlike Radio Sawa, Alhurra TV faces a crowded market and will not easily find a niche. As described above, the Arab television market is intensely

---

25. Kenneth Tomlinson, testimony to Senate Committee on Foreign Relations, *The Broadcasting Board of Governors: Finding the Right Media for the Message in the Middle East.* 108th congress, 2nd session, April 29, 2004. Also see the 2004 Report of the United States Advisory Commission on Public Diplomacy, Department of State, November 2004; "Radio Sawa launches 'Sawa Chat,'" press release, November 15, 2002; and "New Survey Numbers Confirm Radio Sawa's Growth and Popularity in the Middle East," press release, September 25, 2003.

26. Barbara Slavin, "VOA Changes Prompt Staffer Protests," *USA Today*, July 12, 2004.

27. Ibid.

competitive. Alhurra may hope to succeed in the way that Fox News has succeeded: by presenting an unavoidable partisan voice, whose success leads others stations such as CNN and MSNBC to imitate and respond, thereby reshaping the media landscape. But Fox had a large potential audience groomed by conservative talk radio over the years, as well as close ties to the Republican party. Alhurra has no such waiting audience, nor close ties to Arab ruling parties. Unless al Jazeera, al Arabiya, and other stations find themselves losing market share to a pro-American competitor, they seem more likely to ignore it than to imitate it.

Unlike Radio Sawa, Alhurra has not distinguished itself with a superior product. The general response to Alhurra's programming has been tepid. As one Arab writer complains, "Anyone who knows the American media or has worked in Washington will be shocked watching this satellite channel broadcasting at its present standard."[28] While Alhurra's advocates frequently cite its state-of-the-art facilities, few Arab viewers have been especially impressed. While I have not collected any systematic evidence on this, anecdotally I have heard its programs described as boring, tedious, stale, and—most damning—as no different from the programming found on the Arab state-run stations to which al Jazeera offered such a refreshing alternative. The documentaries and other programming are generally seen as uninteresting or even bizarrely out of tune with Arab concerns and interests. And it is worth mentioning that, in contrast to al Jazeera's extremely popular and content-rich Arabic language Web site, which allows users to easily search and retrieve full transcripts of every program over the last five years at no cost, Alhurra has only a rudimentary and content-free Web site.[29]

Perhaps the single moment that crippled Alhurra in the eyes of Arab audiences was its belated response to the Israeli assassination of Hamas leader Shaykh Ahmed Yassin. Every Arab satellite station covered the Palestinian demonstrations and funeral live, while "in contrast, at midday, when many people in the Arab world were watching television to find out what was happening, the U.S. government–financed Arabic-language satellite station Al-Hurra was showing a translated American cooking program."[30] The station learned from this experience and made a point of offering some five hours of coverage of the assassination of Abd al Aziz al Rantissi in late April,

---

28. Tariq al Homayed, "Al-Hurra Channel...Washington's Error," *Arab News*, July 16, 2004.

29. Compare al Jazeera (http://www.aljazeera.net) to Alhurra (http://www.alhurra.com). Al Arabiya (http://www.alarabiya.net) also has an increasingly accessible Web site.

30. Michael Young, "Death in a Wheelchair," *Slate*, March 22, 2004, http://slate.msn.com/id/2097494/. I have heard variations on this anecdote from dozens of Arab interviewees.

but the damage had been done. Given the resources available to Alhurra, which allows it to hire a large and talented staff, it is reasonable to expect that these shortcomings will eventually be rectified; but by then, it may well be too late to reclaim the missed opportunity to capture a market.

One particularly surprising shortcoming of Alhurra has been its weakness in covering American domestic politics. Honestly explaining the American political system to the Arab public, in all of its messiness and contradictions and with a full airing for criticisms of the Bush Administration, could make Alhurra indispensable to Arab audiences. But Alhurra's coverage has fallen short. For example, al Jazeera had more correspondents covering the Democratic National Convention in July 2004 than Alhurra and al Arabiya combined.[31] When Alhurra has covered American politics, its choices have not addressed the issues and questions of most importance to Arab audiences; live coverage of Reagan's funeral, for example, could hardly interest most Arabs. Much of the coverage of American politics focuses on Middle East issues, with only very occasional special reports or roundtables on more general aspects of American politics. Following al Jazeera's precedent, Alhurra began a weekly program on the 2004 elections during the Democratic National Convention. But there is a dilemma: if Alhurra does cover American politics more incisively and aggressively, it will likely find itself coming under Congressional and partisan criticism which could adversely affect its independence and its budget. This is an inevitable problem for a government-run station, one which may well be beyond the ability of even talented staff to correct.

Finally, and most importantly, even if a niche existed, the credibility problem would remain. At the end of the day, Alhurra will not be able to escape the fact that it is an official American government station and will be judged on those terms. In response to the Abu Ghraib prison scandal, for example, Alhurra broadcast a documentary called "Remembering Saddam"—a riveting story of seven men whose hands had been amputated under Saddam—and then showed the men meeting President Bush the next day. What might have been effective programming under other conditions, unfortunately, here gave the impression of propaganda aimed at deflecting criticism of the United States over the prison scandal—reducing its impact and reinforcing skepticism about the station's independence. "Good job," said the president at the end of his May 5 interview with Alhurra, a baffling remark which did nothing for the station's reputation for independence.[32]

---

31. Dante Chinni, "A Very Arab View on Very American Politics," *Christian Science Monitor*, July 29, 2004.

32. President George W. Bush interview with Alhurra, May 5, 2004. Available at www.whitehouse.gov/news/releases/2004/05/20040505-5.htm.

The most important indicator of Alhurra's failure is less what it has or has not done than its total irrelevance. Alhurra has failed to become part of the Arab political conversation. With the exception of President Bush's interview on Abu Ghraib—which largely received negative attention, as Arabs took it as an arrogant snub of al Jazeera—almost no Alhurra program, talk show, event, documentary, or news item has become the subject of serious Arab interest. In contrast to al Jazeera, about which columnists and politicians argue in the Arab media virtually every day, Alhurra comes up in political conversation only as an example of the failures of American policy. James Glassman, a member of the Advisory Commission on Public Diplomacy, told an American Enterprise Institute forum that he had heard from an Egyptian friend that "we will know Alhurra is succeeding when Secretary Powell is besieged with complaints from heads of governments in the world."[33] To date, no such complaints have been registered. This irrelevance to Arab political life is the brutal reality of Alhurra.

Arab Reactions to Alhurra

The first wave of indignant outrage from commentators and calls for boycott from professional associations and political parties was entirely predictable, and as Norman Pattiz argued, gave good publicity to the new station and ensured that many people would tune in to see what the fuss was about.[34] A fatwa by Saudi religious officials against watching Alhurra received some attention, although it should be noted that Saudi religious authorities also issued a fatwa against watching al Jazeera because it "hosts so-called reformists who have a podium for airing their poisonous ideas."[35] One hopes that Alhurra will match al Jazeera in this regard.

While many Arab commentators attacked the new station, others wondered what the fuss was about. The pro-American Kuwaiti Ahmad al Rubi'i chided critics of Alhurra by reminding them that the United States is a rich and powerful state, which has every right to start a television station if it wants to. But, Rubi'i comments, "Alhurra can't hope to succeed if its task is just to whitewash America, or if it loses its credibility, as stations that practice political propaganda will fall into the void and Arabs won't watch them."[36] Abd al Rahman al Rashed, the outspokenly pro-American former

---

33. American Enterprise Institute, "Selling America: How Well Does U.S. Government Broadcasting Work in the Middle East?" forum, May 11, 2004.

34. Norman Pattiz, remarks at George Washington University, February 27, 2004; quoted by Ori Nir, "Network Beams America into Arab Living Rooms," *The Forward*, April 23, 2004.

35. United Press International, *Washington Times*, May 20, 2004.

36. Ahmad al Rubi'i, "A New Satellite Station," *Al Sharq al Awsat*, February 17, 2004.

editor of *al Sharq al Awsat* (and now managing director of al Arabiya), pointed out that American news and opinions have long been available on the Internet, in magazines, or on CNN, and Alhurra will be adding little new.[37] Rashed pointed out that Israel itself has been broadcasting in Arabic for some time and he does not know a single person who changed his mind about Israel because of it.

The more critical *al Quds al Arabi* more or less rolled its eyes at Alhurra:

> The station most reminds us of the official Arab television stations run by dictatorial regimes, with the President as the first guest, just as any official Arab station would be sure to have its king or dictator as the first guest. The interviewer questioned President Bush just as an Arab journalist would question an Arab leader on an official station, protecting him from difficult questions and being sure not to anger his employer.[38]

Munir Shafiq dismissed the idea that the American media are "objective" compared with the Arab media, pointing to American media coverage of Israel and Iraq as examples of highly distorted and biased coverage.[39] Shafiq, like others, warned that Americans were wrong to assume that al Jazeera shaped public opinion and not the other way around. The prominent Egyptian columnist Fahmy Huwaydi pointed out that Latin Americans, Europeans, and Asians did not need al Jazeera to make them resent American policies, and doubted that Alhurra would have any real impact either way.[40] Jamil Nimri observed that the station looks good, professional, and attractive, and that this alone might put it into the second rank of Arab satellites…since "Arabs won't automatically reach for the remote when they see it."[41] He thinks that viewers will not necessarily turn it off just because it is American, and if they see interesting talk shows or programs, it could arouse interest. Arab listeners never boycotted the BBC, after all, despite their differences with British policy. But Nimri argues that Arabs have long been experienced at reading between the lines of official discourse. Arabs tuned out official Arab television, and they will tune out an official American station for the same reason.

---

37. Abd al Rahman al Rashed, "Why This Campaign against Alhurra?" *Al Sharq al Awsat*, February 19, 2004.

38. *Al Quds al Arabi*, editorial, February 17, 2004.

39. Munir Shafiq, "Alhurra and the Illusion of Objectivity," *Al Rai*, February 1, 2004.

40. Fahmy Huwaydi, *Al Sharq al Awsat*, February 21, 2004.

41. Jamil Nimri, "Alhurra in the Satellite Marketplace," *Al Arab al Yom*, February 17, 2004.

Fahd al Fanik pointed out that American criticism of the Arab media as government funded rings hollow since Alhurra is itself government funded.[42]   Similarly, Samih al Mayateh said that America's calls for democracy and opening do not sit well with the media model offered by Alhurra, which looks more like "the official media of a totalitarian state, whose owners betray their own lack of confidence in it by giving it the name 'The Free One.'"[43]   How can the Americans demand a free media for Arabs, he asked, when Alhurra "entrenches the idea of a state media... imitating them in their coverage of the kings and princes." Yasir al Za'atra declared Alhurra to be a stillborn project, that will be able to attract only a very limited audience.[44]   By March, Rakan al Majali concluded that of all the Arab satellite stations, "it is possible to say that Alhurra is the least important and least influential on Arab public opinion."[45]

Public Diplomacy

Alhurra will not necessarily be a fiasco. It could have some small benefits, if well done. Given the very real importance of satellite television in contemporary Arab politics, it cannot hurt to have an American voice in the region. However, if that voice lacks credibility, or if it attracts few viewers, then its utility will be minimal. Rather than being actively harmful, it is more likely that Alhurra will continue to be irrelevant, a costly white elephant that drives out other, more potentially effective elements of public diplomacy. Alhurra's budget of $62 million represents almost 10 percent of the State Department's budget for public diplomacy; only $25 million is allocated for public diplomacy outreach programs for the entire Arab and Muslim world. With Alhurra sapping up scarce resources, proposals such as establishing American Centers, increasing the number and training of public diplomacy staff, and directly engaging with opinion leaders have languished. In May 2004, Margaret Tutwiler resigned as undersecretary for public diplomacy and public affairs after only six months, leaving that crucial position vacant once again.

Beyond these budgetary issues, however, is the underlying philosophy that proffers Alhurra as the centerpiece of American public diplomacy. Christopher Ross, special coordinator for public diplomacy for the State Department, elegantly explained that "public diplomacy engages

---

42. Fahd al Fanik, "The American Station Alhurra," *Al Rai,* February 17, 2004.
43. Samih al Mayateh, "Alhurra is Bound by American Policy and Loses Its Credibility," *Al Arab al Yom,* February 18, 2004.
44. Yasir al Za'atra, "From Alhurra to the Greater Middle East," *Al Dustour,* February 17, 2004.
45. Rakan al Majali, *Al Dustour,* March 1, 2004.

carefully targeted sectors of foreign publics in order to develop support for [American] strategic goals." Similarly, the Council on Foreign Relations Task Force on Public Diplomacy recommended "increas[ing] customized, 'two-way' dialogue, as contrasted to conventional one-way 'push-down' mass communication, including an 'engagement' approach that involves listening, dialogue, and debate…that fosters meaningful relationships between U.S. and foreign journalists."[46] A Brookings report on U.S. policy towards the Islamic world makes a similar point: "public diplomacy will be most effective and persuasive when it is rooted in a dialogue between American and foreign civil society."[47] This is precisely what Alhurra does not do, and in some ways works against. The Advisory Commission on Public Diplomacy offered an impressive array of suggestions for implementing the kind of public diplomacy Ross recommended, but the Bush Administration has shown little interest. Saying that we are engaged in a "battle of ideas," as is fashionable, has the unfortunate implication of a conflictual relationship, one in which "our" ideas must defeat "theirs."[48] But such martial metaphors are not conducive to genuine dialogue.

A far better approach to public diplomacy would be to fundamentally change the way we approach Arab public opinion, particularly the influential elites whose voices reach millions of Arabs through the existing Arab media. In particular, there exists a class of opinion makers—journalists, television personalities, independent politicians—who are fiercely critical of the Arab status quo and who share many of the professed goals of the Bush Administration: greater democracy, economic reform, accountability, and public freedoms. These people have great influence over the terms of debate in the Arab world, far more than do the individuals to which the United States too often prefers as its interlocutors in the region. Most of these opinion makers are critical of the United States and Israel, and on these grounds have been treated more as adversaries than as potential partners. The only way that the United States will be able to engage these people effectively is to drop its assumption that its policies are not subject to discussion, and that the only role of Arab intellectuals is to support (or oppose) them.

This is the heart and soul of public diplomacy: persuasion through rational argument, in direct intercourse with influential opinion leaders, rather than attempts to manipulate mass audiences through television

---

46. *Public Diplomacy: A Strategy for Reform*, report of the Independent Task Force on Public Diplomacy. (Washington, DC: Council on Foreign Relations, 2002).

47. Hady Amr, *The Need to Communicate: How to Improve U.S. Public Diplomacy with the Islamic World* (Washington DC: The Brookings Institution, 2004).

48. Marc Lynch, "Taking Arabs Seriously," *Foreign Affairs* 82 (5): 81–94.

broadcasting that ignores and antagonizes those opinion leaders. Alienating them—as the United States has been doing seemingly as a matter of principle for the last couple of years—is self-defeating: it both loses the chance to harness a potential ally, and it strengthens the hostility of those with the greatest influence over public opinion. As much as the new Arab media challenges American foreign policy in the region, it challenges the repressive status quo in the Arab world far more. If the Bush Administration is serious about promoting Arab reform, then it should recognize its potential allies for change from within.

Alhurra's best hope for winning an audience would be to broadcast hard-hitting programming about the missing Iraqi weapons of mass destruction, about Bush's domestic political problems, and about American foreign policy. It should air frequent and uncompromising investigations of human rights abuses and political reform dilemmas of American allies such as Egypt, Jordan, and Saudi Arabia, and not only those of less friendly states such as Syria. It should cover American politics thoroughly, using its comparative advantage to offer something other stations cannot match. Such programming would help it to win credibility, would make it interesting to Arabs, and would be a concrete demonstration that the American idea of a free press really is more than propaganda. Stephen Cook of the Council on Foreign Relations proposes transforming Alhurra into a kind of C-Span, focusing on coverage of American politics.[49] But in any case, it is vital to shed the illusion that American Arabic-language broadcasting will have a significant effect on American policy problems or on anti-Americanism in the region.

---

49. Steven Cook, "Hearts, Minds, and Hearings," *New York Times,* July 6, 2004.

8. Academic and Professional Exchanges with the Islamic World: An Undervalued Tool

Barry Ballow

You don't judge public diplomacy's effectiveness in the span of months or even years; it's a long-term effort whose result you see over the course of generations. It is also a long-term proposition that we are dedicated to, that we've never lost sight of.

—State Department spokesman, July 2004

For nearly sixty years, through numerous political changes in Congress and the White House, one element of American foreign policy has continued to perform with dependable effectiveness, providing strong and dynamic underpinning for the conduct of political, economic, and cultural relations with the rest of the world: academic, professional, and cultural exchanges. Over these six decades, hundreds of thousands of highly qualified foreign and U.S. students, teachers, scholars, and professionals have participated in U.S. government-sponsored people-to-people exchanges. In turn, these exchanges have fostered countless continuing international connections through dialogue and collaboration, promoted more enlightened thinking, and encouraged deeper and lasting international understanding. Through exchanges, Americans have become more globally literate and have contributed to the nation's security. Foreign visitors have experienced first hand the best qualities of this country through contact with common citizens and local communities. They have also learned about how Americans deal with their issues and problems.

A great many exchange participants, foreign and American, have gone on to become important figures in their countries and on the global scene. Thousands have won leadership roles in government; others are playing dominant roles in science, business, the arts, and education. At least thirty-two have become Nobel Prize laureates, with countless others winning national and international recognition for contributions to their professions or to the global commonweal. The positive impact of exchanges has endured even in times and places where U.S. foreign policy is strongly opposed and faces open hostility. This is nowhere more true than in the Islamic world of 2004.

> *First of all, Syrians aren't terrorists; second, your policy toward Israel and Palestine is not a fair one and causes you many problems in this region; third, we need to vastly increase the number of Syrian students going to the U.S., but also the number of Americans coming to Syria. It's the best way to build our bilateral relationship and resolve our differences.*
>
> —Syrian university president

In the wake of the 9/11 attacks, an increasingly intense, often acrimonious, national debate has evolved on the role of public diplomacy in the struggle against world terrorism and growing anti-Americanism, particularly in the Middle East and broader Islamic world. Most participants in the discussion, particularly members of Congress, public intellectuals, and public affairs professionals, charge that the federal government's public diplomacy apparatus has been deficient in connecting with Islamic societies, particularly with the younger populations in those states. The recently released report of the bipartisan 9/11 Commission joined that chorus of critics by laying out a harsh critique of the federal government's public diplomacy efforts since the attacks.

Criticism has often focused on the method as well as the message. Advertisements in Arab media extolling shared personal values; a focus on popular culture in new, U.S. government-sponsored Arab-language broadcasting; and a glitzy Arab-language youth magazine produced by the State Department have all been criticized for a variety of perceived shortcomings, including lack of substance. At the same time, I think it is fair to say that in most countries of the Middle East and in a good part of the rest of the Islamic world, the proverbial 800-pound gorilla lurking in the corner—American policy vis-à-vis the Israelis and Palestinians—overshadows or diminishes the very important U.S. message on the global impact of terrorism.

In lamenting the lost effectiveness of U.S. public diplomacy, many critics point to the demise of the U.S. Information Agency (USIA) and argue that the decline in effectiveness of public diplomacy began when USIA was absorbed by the Department of State in 1999. Some propose the unlikely reestablishment of the former independent agency or urge, at the least, that traditional USIA programs and services such as American libraries and cultural centers be reconstituted throughout the Middle East and the rest of the Islamic world.

Tellingly, there are virtually no voices now arguing that our public diplomacy structure is adequate to the current task of countering the immense anti-American sentiments that have grown over the past ten years—becoming virulent toward the end of 2004—in the Middle East and other parts of the Islamic world.

Public Diplomacy professionals, some members of Congress and staffers, and many foreign affairs experts predicted the slide in effectiveness of public diplomacy as far back as the mid-1990s, when a post-Cold War foreign policy was still evolving and an official public interface with the rest of the world didn't seem very important to many in the Congress who were earnestly chiseling away at USIA's annual appropriations. American libraries and cultural centers, cultural presentations, book translations, news services, English language programs and publications were eliminated or scaled back to minimal size.

> TELLINGLY, THERE ARE VIRTUALLY NO VOICES NOW ARGUING THAT OUR PUBLIC DIPLOMACY STRUCTURE IS ADEQUATE TO THE CURRENT TASK OF COUNTERING THE IMMENSE ANTI-AMERICAN SENTIMENTS THAT HAVE GROWN IN THE MIDDLE EAST AND OTHER PARTS OF THE ISLAMIC WORLD.

Today, among what remains of U.S.-friendly or simply moderate voices in Muslim countries and elsewhere—there are many people who will tie their appreciation for or understanding of the United States to some early experience in a U.S. Information Service Library or cultural center or, very often, to time spent in the United States as a student, official visitor, or classroom teacher.

The strongest admirers of the United States, and those who generally understand us best, are typically those who spent months or years in the United States as students, teachers, or research scholars. These individuals, selected for exchange programs because of their intellectual and leadership qualities, have usually established enduring relationships with American colleagues, institutions, and communities.

And therein, I would argue, lies the good news in what might otherwise be viewed as a bleak picture with little hope for improvement in the short term. The most effective form of soft diplomacy—academic and professional exchanges—continues and produces important results by showcasing American society and values for important audiences who are invited to this country as official guests of the American people. Positive impressions endure in spite of unhappiness with U.S. policies in the Middle East, the war in Iraq, disputes with long-term allies, and battles over specific trade issues. Exchanges have also given Americans opportunities to acquire knowledge of other cultures and societies that are critically important to this country's knowledge base.

The fact is that U.S. government-sponsored exchanges have chugged on productively outside the political fray with the strong encouragement and support (some of it substantial financial support) of 160 governments, many of whom have serious concurrent issues with the United States. The historic success of exchanges, leading to financial buy-in by partner governments in the case of the Fulbright Program, has made these activities an integral and important part of the U.S. relationship with those governments. In some 51 countries, the Fulbright Program is actually based on a negotiated bilateral agreement that is the result of a shared decision by both governments to deepen and make more visible the extent of their political relationship.

> *I think your government has not lived up to its responsibilities in the Middle East and I condemn it for that, but I have witnessed how this country's democratic institutions work in a small American community and I want that success for my country.*
>
> —Algerian Fulbright Senior Scholar, 2001

While the Fulbright Program can boast of a well-established network of partners overseas and in the United States, the International Visitor Program and Citizen Exchanges Program can also point with pride to a vast, nationwide volunteer base in the United States numbering some 80,000 people and hundreds of organizations that are the foundation of those programs.

Since the late 1940s, the U.S. Department of State and the former U.S. Information Agency have sponsored more than 750,000 individuals in people-to-people exchanges. These programs include the venerable Fulbright Scholarship Programs—the U.S. government flagship exchange activity and template for many other similar, specialized programs—which sponsors the exchange of some 5,000 foreign and American participants annually. Through the short-term (three-week) International Visitor Program and a range of institution-to-institution programs that involve many citizens' organizations in the United States and abroad, the State Department also brings hundreds of foreign participants into meaningful professional contact with American counterparts. In 2003, an American Speakers program sent more than 700 U.S. experts abroad to speak about specific policy issues and binational concerns.

Over many years, the Agency for International Development, the Department of Education, the Department of Health and Human Resources, and some fifty other federal agencies have also sponsored tens of thousands of exchange programs related to development, science, medicine, and a very wide spectrum of other subjects.

A great strength of sponsored academic and professional exchanges has been its emphasis on the selection of proven or potential leaders, on the assumption that they are individuals who are likely to take full advantage of the experience and share what they have learned in the United States with their compatriots, A second strength has been the U.S. government's forgoing a direct focus on policy messages and short-term policy goals. From the beginning, sponsored exchanges were designed to foster mutual understanding and long-term engagement with potentially influential individuals on a global scale. These exchanges have generated tolerance and appreciation of foreign values, culture, and institutions, as well as lasting connections between exchange participants and their hosts.

> *Fulbright provided me the bridge to cross. I saw how things can be done differently in a different society. I learned lessons which stood in good stead when building up the micro-credit structure of the Grameen Bank.*
> —Bangladeshi Fulbright Student, 1965

Anyone who has administered educational and professional exchange programs has heard countless foreign exchange participants express their deep appreciation for the workings of American democracy at the local and national levels, for the pervasiveness of the American work ethic, and for the enduring potential for upward mobility within American society. They can recount many stories of grantees returning home with the spoken desire to build similar institutions and with a commitment to maintain strong private, personal ties with American colleagues.

> *The U.S. brought me to America as a Fulbrighter. That was an important experience in my life. We decided to send our children to the U.S. for their higher education. I think that's only fair.*
> —A former prime minister of Yemen

Exchanges have frequently led to productive connections between visitors and their U.S. host institutions. This is increasingly true as the Internet allows contacts and friendships made during a face-to-face encounter to ripen into collaborative relationships after the exchange participant has returned home. More specifically, American leaders frequently find themselves dealing with foreign leaders who have been official or unofficial visitors in the United States. These foreign leaders bring to any discussion or negotiation an understanding of—if not agreement with—U.S. positions. Their grasp of the United States advances the starting point for these interfaces, averts basic misunderstandings, and promotes a positive conclusion to bilateral discussions on any subject.

Since the late 1940s, countries of the Middle East, South Asia, and Islamic states in Asia and Africa have participated in U.S. government-sponsored exchange programs. Between 1948 and 2002, some 6,600 participants from the Middle East alone had done graduate study in the United States, had undertaken postgraduate research, or had taught in U.S. secondary schools and universities through the Fulbright Program. That number is approximately one-tenth the total of grantees for the same program categories from western and central Europe, but given the limited support provided by partner governments in the Middle East—only Morocco and Jordan have made significant contributions to exchange funding—and the number of countries and states who have been cut off from or have had limited access to the program through the years—Algeria, Iraq, Kuwait, Lebanon, Libya, Sudan, West Bank/Gaza and Yemen—the lesser figures are understandable.

For Middle Eastern visitors to the United States, a lengthy exchange experience can demonstrate how elements of Western democratic society can be usefully adapted to the Islamic cultural context in ways that respect the critical need to maintain the latter.

It has been argued that Middle Easterners tend to believe that American democracy is entirely about protecting the rights of the individual without reference or respect for the group values that are more the norm in Islamic society. The first-hand experience of an exchange visit in the United States can allow the Arab visitor to see just how important community and family—two central aspects of Middle Eastern society—are in this country. Typically, Middle Easterners in the United States have been particularly impressed with the extent of volunteerism and community service that are common and important in U.S. society.

> *I plan to present a better understanding of American society in my public speeches, writing, and seminars, and [to] enhance interfaith dialogues.*
> —Indonesian International Visitor Program participant, 2003

Academic exchanges with Islamic South Asia, including Bangladesh, India, the Maldives, and Pakistan, have been significant since the 1950s. But there have been prolonged absences from the program by Afghanistan, Iran, and Pakistan. These partner governments have provided virtually no financial support for bilateral exchanges, although they have always seen exchanges as beneficial and have warmly welcomed them.

Since the 1950s, the State Department's International Visitor Program has brought thousands of professionals from Islamic countries to the United States. These short-term programs have been somewhat easier to develop and implement even during periods of political and social unrest. The selection process for the program generally involves the entire U.S. embassy mission. Invitations are frequently extended to rising political and economic leaders on the brink of taking authority in their countries. These programs, which connect the visitors with U.S. counterparts and expose them to American institutions, result in well-informed interlocutors for political, economic, and other important bilateral discussions.

But what of exchange programs since September 2001? Have they been able to help the U.S. government overcome its lack of credibility in the Islamic world?

If it is true that public opinion in Arab and Muslim countries responds more to policies than to public diplomacy, it is clear that successful public diplomacy will not be able to change minds dramatically in the presence of strong opposition to policy.[1]

The State Department, and more specifically, the Bureau of Educational and Cultural Affairs (ECA) under its current assistant secretary, can make a credible claim to foresight and enlightened response to the current crisis in relations with the Islamic world. Since the attacks of September 2001, ECA has redirected considerable resources to programs for and with Muslim countries and has developed new exchanges that serve the particular needs of the Islamic world. The number of participants in State Department-sponsored programs from the Middle East and South Asia doubled between 2000 and 2003, jumping from 1,152 to 2,358, and the Department projects further increases for 2004 and beyond.

As early as 2000, the ECA had begun to shift program priorities in the direction of the Middle East with an eye to the festering problem of the Israeli-Palestinian conflict. For example, within the Fulbright Foreign Student and Scholar Programs, ECA established a conflict resolution component that brought Arabs and Israelis together for a study program focused on resolving issues at the community level. The success of the first program led to the creation of separate two-year courses for South Asians and Africans and a repeat of the program for Middle Easterners.

---

1. Edward P. Djerejian, *Changing Minds, Winning Peace: A New Strategic Direction for U.S. Public Diplomacy in the Arab and Muslim World,* report of the Advisory Group on Public Diplomacy for the Arab and Muslim World (Washington, DC: 2003), 66.

Recognizing the dearth of foreign language study programs in U.S. higher education and a consequent lack of American language and area expertise—particularly for the Middle East—ECA sponsored a new Arabic language component of the Fulbright Foreign Language Teaching Assistant Program (FLTA) in early 2001. Beginning with five participants in 2001, FLTA's immediate success with U.S. universities and colleges and with participants themselves led to its rapid expansion to include young participants speaking Bengali, Hausa, Hindi, Bahasa Indonesian, Swahili, Turkish, Urdu, and Uzbek. The program now provides opportunities for young teachers of English in nearly twenty Muslim countries to teach their mother languages at U.S. colleges and universities, with an emphasis on smaller regional institutions, while taking coursework in U.S. studies. These young teachers are also proactively integrated into local American communities. After an academic year, they return to their home countries and English-teaching positions with refined teaching skills, better English proficiency, and a deepened understanding of American values and society. ECA expects to place approximately 100 FLTA participants nationwide in 2005.

In 2001, the Fulbright U.S. Student Program added an Islamic Civilization component to enable American graduate students and newly graduated BA students to enhance their knowledge and understanding of Islam and Islamic history and culture through overseas research in countries with significant Muslim populations. The program's basic goal is to enlarge the U.S. knowledge base of the Islamic world. Rather counterintuitively, this new Fulbright Student Program has also rapidly expanded despite continuing conflict and violence in areas where participants may opt to do their research.

After 9/11, ECA began to evaluate all of its exchange programs for their potential worth in bridging the growing understanding gap with the peoples of the Muslim world. A December 2001 conference in Morocco sponsored by AMIDEAST provided ECA with the opportunity to unveil a revised programming approach to the Islamic world—Partnerships for Learning (P4L). The Partnerships rubric includes all of the ECA's activities oriented toward Muslim countries—exchanges for students, scholars, teachers, professionals, as well as English teaching activities and cultural presentations—many in new or tailored formats. Five basic goals for the new programming approach are: (1) to develop a dialogue with moderates in Muslim countries; (2) to broaden American understanding of Islam and of countries that are predominantly Islamic; (3) to reach more people with accurate information about the United States and deepen their understanding through personal experiences with Americans; (4) to increase foreign understanding and acceptance of U.S. goals; and (5) to engage successor generations.   While none of these goals is particularly new to sponsored programs—there have been programs oriented toward successor generations since the 1960s, for example—the objectives do appear particularly appropriate in attempting to reach disaffected Muslims around the world.

Importantly, ECA's initiative resonated well with U.S. missions in the field, which generally favor the tried and true, or at least the logical. Changes in policy and programming paths developed by Washington are not always received with enthusiasm by the experts overseas.   In my experience, another Department initiative, the Middle East Program Initiative, has had a much rockier beginning partly due to Washington's frequent changes of policy course, its reluctance to collaborate with field partners in program design, and its slowness in making program funding available.

> *Muslims in the West… have greater freedom to debate the future of their faith. Islam in America now is safer than in its lands of origin, where the impulse of the power structure is to control Islam and manipulate it for political use. [In the U.S.] Islam is free to be Islam.*
>
> —Egyptian Fulbright Senior Scholar, 2000

With the beginning of the 2002 program year, ECA began to redirect 5 percent of its annual budget to Partnership for Learning programs oriented toward the Muslim world. Since FY 2002, ECA has dedicated over $40 million dollars to this new initiative. ECA requested an additional $25 million for Partnership for Learning for FY 2005, which would increase funding for the P4L initiative to over $65 million.[2] All of this will go to the Arab and Muslim worlds.

The Partnership for Learning Initiative has developed into a widening spectrum of exchange activities. For example, since 2002, under P4L, the International Visitor Program has brought to the United States a growing number of current and emerging Muslim leaders representing national and local governments, NGOs, media, and civic and religious groups from nineteen countries. The visitors participate in tailor-made programs that put them directly in touch with American counterparts and allow them to assess for themselves how this country approaches issues related to an independent media, foreign policy formulation, religion and politics, and conflict resolution.

---

2. In early 2003, Congress stipulated that 24 percent of ECA program funds were to be spent for activities in the Middle East and South Asia. This requirement is expected to continue in FY2005.

In addition, the Bureau established a new Middle East, North Africa, and Indonesia youth exchange program, Youth and Exchange and Study (YES), which brought 170 Muslim students to the United States in 2003. In 2004, YES plans to extend the reach of the program to the south, central, and Southeast Asia areas and to increase the number of participants to 480. By the 2006-2007 school year, ECA hopes to have 1,000 high school students from the Arab and Muslim worlds studying side-by-side with American youths. The program is greatly assisted through the volunteerism of hundreds of Muslim-American host families.

The Bureau also expanded English teaching activities, dispatching ESL experts and teaching materials to more countries in the Muslim world.

The Partnerships for Learning Undergraduate Study Program (PLUS) provides English language training and two-year scholarships for Arab students to complete undergraduate study in the United States. This new scholarship program focuses on the recruitment of non-elite, gifted young men and women who would otherwise have no opportunity for foreign study and first-hand exposure to the United States. The first PLUS group of 70 students from 12 Arab countries arrived in the United States in February 2004. The program will expand to 100 participants in 2005 and include students from South Asia.

Further, ECA developed new American studies summer institutes for university students from the Middle East and South Asia that provide intensive, five-week courses in American values, culture, society, and institutions at a regional American college or university campus. Beyond the academic component, participants are given the opportunity to interact with community organizations and spend time with American families. More than a hundred participants are expected in 2005.

> *When I was preparing to come here, some of my friends told me that Americans are very hostile and they are anti-Arab and [anti-]Muslim. So, along with the two heavy suitcases I brought with me, I brought a lot of wrong notions and ideas about this country. That was the first adjustment I had to go through.*
>
> —PLUS Undergraduate Student, 2004

The Fulbright program was extended with the establishment of an Islamic Specialist Program that brings senior academics from Muslim countries to lecture and consult at U.S. colleges and universities on Islamic culture, society, and institutions for two to six weeks, and it revived exchange programs with Afghanistan, Iraq, and Libya and created a new set of exchanges with the republic of the Maldives.

From what I have observed in American society, in terms of political and social change—especially when contemplating the civil rights movement of the 1960s—I think I need to be an evolutionary leader, not a revolutionary one, when I return home. Changing the attitudes of Iraqis and Middle Easterners is more important than changing political systems. Thus, I have a dream to see Iraq and other Middle Eastern leaders advocating change not through bloodshed, violence, and hatred but by advocating peace and love.

—Iraqi Fulbright Student, 2004

Literally weeks after the Taliban regime was chased into the mountains of Afghanistan in 2002, plans to restore the Fulbright Program in that country were underway. In early 2004, the first Afghan participants in the Fulbright Student Program arrived at their assigned American universities to begin programs of study.

Within days of the fall of Baghdad to American-led forces, the Provisional Authority was requesting the restoration of the Fulbright Program in Iraq—which was suspended in the mid-1970s—and the development of new exchange programs for Iraqi students, scholars, and professionals that would re-establish their connections with the rest of the world. By July 2003 there were twenty Iraqi undergraduates participating in an American studies program in Illinois. A training program at the Smithsonian Institution for Iraqi museum specialists, mostly from the looted Iraq National Museum, was underway by February 2004. Two weeks later, the first group of Iraqi university students arrived for assignment to American colleges and universities, where they are pursuing degrees in liberal arts and the humanities.

The ECA also moved quickly to re-establish educational and cultural exchange programs with Libya in mid-2004. In this effort, they received strong encouragement and support from the Libyan alumni of American universities who had studied in the United States in the 1970s and 1980s, demonstrating once again the lasting effect of exchange programs in building long-term engagement. The revived Libyan exchanges will focus on conflict resolution, public health, and education for the first few years of the program.

The aftermath of 9/11 brought a new emphasis on security and a stringent review process for all visa applications, including those for invited participants in U.S. government-sponsored exchange programs. The new system, known as SEVIS, has slowed the visa process down, discouraged potential participants from applying for U.S.-based programs, forced changes in the recruitment and selection calendar, and increased administrative costs for exchange programs. To date, the new system has not fatally damaged sponsored programs. There have been some would-be participants who have ultimately been turned down for visas by the Department of Homeland Security, or who simply have not had the patience to wait out the review process. It is fair to say that security procedures make it much more difficult and expensive for sponsored exchange programs to keep up with the demands made on them to promote better connections and understanding with the Islamic world.

> *If you offered any one of the young men in that (anti-American) demonstration a chance to study in America, he would quit that mob instantly to accept your offer.*
>
> —Egyptian journalist, 2003

The damage inflicted by new security procedures has been far more severe for students attempting to follow private or non-U.S. government-sponsored study programs. By the 2003-2004 academic year, the foreign student population in the United States stood at 572,509, a drop of nearly 14,000 over the previous year. This was the first net decrease in international enrollments in many years. According to the Institute of International Education, which tracks international education trends using a well-developed network of U.S. universities and colleges, a 5 percent overall drop in undergraduate registrations was partially offset by a 2.5 percent increase in the number of foreign graduate students.[3]

An even more worrisome development in 2003-2004 was the continuing decline in students coming from the Middle East and other Islamic countries. In the past year, Arab student numbers were down 9 percent overall. This drop followed a similar decline in 2002-2003 of 10 percent. Students from the Middle East now account for only 6 percent of all international students enrolled in U.S. higher education. There were also fewer students from the important Muslim countries of Turkey (down 2 percent), Indonesia (down 15 percent), and Pakistan (down 10 percent). There are no indications that the downward trend might level off in the short term.

These non-U.S. government funded students are not only important in building bridges of understanding between Americans and other peoples, they also make substantial financial ($13 billion per year), intellectual, and cultural contributions to the United States that American higher education

---

3. IIE, *Open Doors 2004: International Students in the U.S.*, Washington, DC: Institute of International Education.

and its surrounding communities have come to count on heavily in recent years. Foreign student enrollment declines, if they continue, will hurt local economies, make research and development of all kinds more difficult, and stifle knowledge acquisition of other countries and cultures nationwide.

Educational and professional exchanges have worked extraordinarily well in building and maintaining meaningful dialogue between the United States and the rest of the world through the years of the Cold War, the post-colonial period in the developing world, the Vietnam War era, and the evolution of a new Europe and Eurasia. For those sixty years, they have provided precisely the platform for understanding that is now needed to repair and build U.S. relationships with the peoples of the Muslim world.

> *What Washington can and must do is continue fund programs like Fulbright to bring Muslim students, particularly women, to the United States. Many of them, after all, will be important voices when they return home.*
> —Malaysian Fulbright Scholar, 2002

Yet, despite their recognized value and the praise that has been heaped upon them by Congress, the Executive Branch, the U.S. private sector, foreign governments and institutions, and most of all, by program participants, they remain woefully underutilized and underfunded.[4] Many of these financial difficulties began in the 1990s and continue into the present. As post-Cold War public diplomacy in general sought credibility within the Clinton Administration and from the various elements of Congress responsible for program authorization and funding—people who were already somewhat ambivalent about public diplomacy—a significant political change in the form of the "Contract with America" arrived on the political scene with the elections of 1994. The new priorities that came with the Republican Congress of 1995 saw all federal programs, including

---

4. A serious challenge to maintaining robust global public diplomacy exchange programs was the rather unexpected 1999 merger of the U.S. Information Agency into the State Department. This shotgun marriage was not welcomed by either USIA or State Department career professionals, who saw many basic incompatibilities in the coupling. Particularly worrisome to the managers of USIA's "soft diplomacy" programs, which traditionally aimed at long-term engagement and the steady building of mutual understanding, was the sudden need to co-exist and compete within an organization more typically preoccupied with short-term policy issues and goals. Congress itself apparently had some qualms about the deal, as it ultimately stipulated that exchange programs would have their own allocation line in the annual appropriations legislation. Since 2000, funding for the ECA, which was transferred to the State Department virtually intact from the former USIA, has been isolated from the rest of the State Department's allocation, which effectively prevents poaching in the budget process.

educational and professional exchanges, absorb massive funding cuts in 1996 and 1997.

There has been no significant increase in base funding for the Fulbright Program, the International Visitor Program, or the Citizen Exchanges Program since 1994. On the contrary, Congress reduced funding for the respected Fulbright Program (which had originated as a Congressional initiative), by nearly 30 percent, from $125 million in 1994 to $95 million in 1996. The perennially successful International Visitor Program and Citizen Exchanges experienced even deeper cuts in their smaller budgets. It has taken nearly ten years for funding for all of these well-respected programs to modestly rebound. The budget for the Fulbright Program in FY 2004 was $131 million—still below its 1994 high point when adjusted for inflation and currency fluctuations. Fulbright's binational nature and strong partnership structure were critical during the leanest budget years. Some partner governments and the U.S. and foreign private sectors significantly increased their contributions during this period. Fulbright programs are currently receiving approximately $31 million a year from foreign partner governments and about $74 million from private-sector sources.

> *Wherever we went—from Egypt to Senegal to Turkey—we heard that exchange programs are the single most effective means to improve attitudes toward the United States.*[5]

Given the historical context of the State Department's efforts, some readers may view the program numbers cited in this essay as respectable, but in the context of what now needs to be done in the Muslim world—and on a global basis for that matter—they are wholly inadequate and unimpressive.

Exchange programs are a proven asset that must be used to their maximum potential. The range of U.S. government-sponsored programs' current network of administrative partnerships—which include a dedicated and experienced staff within the Bureau of Educational and Cultural Affairs, equally talented and dedicated private-sector cooperating agencies, a network of tens of thousands of volunteers all over the United States, support from U.S. higher education and thousands of private-sector institutions, and a large group of well-established cooperating organizations all over the globe—should allow the number of participants to double relatively easily and quickly with only moderate staff increases. What is

---

5. Djerejian, 47.

missing for the needed expansion is, of course, program funding. The United States currently spends about the same amount on public diplomacy as do the much smaller countries of Britain and France. There are no such similarities in the amounts the three countries spend on defense.

Shifting program funding earmarked for other regions to programs for the Muslim world is no solution. All regions are important to the United States in one context or another, and the U.S. government can ill-afford to neglect its long-term relationships with any country. Robbing Peter to pay Paul is ultimately a self-defeating approach to foreign relations.

While anti-Americanism runs rampant in the world, and particularly in the Muslim world, one of our best foreign affairs tools remains underutilized. Decision makers in Washington know that educational and academic exchanges can counteract—even prevent—growing hostility toward the United States and Americans, yet they have failed to provide the needed resources to fully exploit that resource. Until they do, this highly valuable foreign relations tool will continue to serve the country, but its impact will be only a fraction of its potential.

9. Reasonable and Proportional Security Measures on International Academic Exchange Programs

Cresencio Arcos

The events of 9/11 marked a watershed in public and government attitudes toward visas and foreign students. Anger that terrorists had entered the United States on student visas was understandable, and frustration at the Immigration and Naturalization Service's inability to account for the number of foreign students—indeed to issue legal adjustments of status to two of the suicide hijackers after the attack—was palpable. California Senator Dianne Feinstein hastily called for a moratorium on all student visas. Other proposals followed. Within a year of the attack, eighteen major executive, legislative, and regulatory changes affecting international visitors were proposed or implemented. Two years later, there were over ninety immigration-related legislative proposals introduced into Congress, mostly motivated by a desire to strengthen the borders.

Regardless of the merits of the individual proposals, the wide public debate they engendered and the reforms adopted created an impression overseas that the United States no longer welcomed foreign visitors. Not everyone argued for the total banning of foreign visitors as did a few opinions and editorials in the daily press, but a survey of subject lines painted the same general picture: screening for foreign students would be heightened and there would be closer tabs on their whereabouts and status. The consequences were not surprising.

As reported by the American Association for the Advancement of Science, various surveys conducted since 2001 indicated declines in the number of foreign students enrolling in U.S. colleges and universities.[1]

---

1. See, for example, American Council on Education Association and others, "Survey of Applications by Prospective International Students to U.S. Higher Education Institutions," Feb. 2004, http://tinyurl.com/68kqs; and Michael Arnone, "New Survey Confirms Sharp Drop in Applications to U.S. Colleges from Foreign Graduate Students," *The Chronicle of Higher Education*, March 4, 2004.

State Department statistics also confirm a general 30 percent decline in visa applications.[2] Anecdotal comments reinforced the concern that the decline was due in some measure to foreign students' fears that they were being targeted. A United Arab Emirates official assigned to Washington, D.C., reported that government-sponsored foreign scholars in the United States dropped from 1,800 to 600 because Arab and Muslim students feared they were being singled out for special treatment, and also because of the "hassle factor" involved in applying for visas.[3]

Another Arab diplomat objectively observed during a meeting with Department of Homeland Security (DHS) officials that the strong American reaction and forceful measures implemented to secure the American homeland were understandable.   Each country sets its own standards, he noted, but he also suggested that it was worthwhile to dispassionately discuss whether the measures remain "reasonable and proportional" to the security problems faced by the United States three years after 9/11. In this regard, it is useful to note one generally unnoticed recommendation by the 9/11 Commission:

> The burden of proof for retaining a particular governmental power should be on the executive, to explain (a) that the power actually materially enhances security and (b) that there is adequate supervision of the executive's use of the powers to ensure protection of civil liberties. If the power is granted, there must be adequate guidelines and oversight to properly confine its use.[4]

This discussion focuses on three topics affecting exchange students: (1) SEVIS, a system to manage information on students and exchange visitors in the United States; (2) NSEERS, a series of measures that required nationals from primarily Arab and Muslim countries to register their entry in and departure from the United States, and a separate entry/exit

---

2. Statistics compiled by the Consular Affairs Bureau indicated that nonimmigrant visa workloads dropped across all categories from 10.347 million in FY 2001 to 6.771 million in FY 2003.

3. An Arab diplomat used the phrase "hassle factor" to refer to the range of difficulties faced in applying for a U.S. visa, which include obtaining an interview appointment, standing in lines for the interview, gathering the documents and forms, paying fees in prescribed methods, undergoing background and security checks, submitting to secondary checks at ports of entry and upon boarding, and registering and re-registering as required by NSEERS.

4. National Commission on Terrorist Attacks upon the United States, *The 9/11 Commission Report*, (Washington, DC: GPO, 2004), 394-395.

program called US-VISIT; and (3) IPASS, an agency conceived to protect sensitive technology and knowledge from being abused by foreign students and scholars and, in relation to IPASS objectives, the impact of State Department clearance policies.

SEVIS

The Enhanced Border Security and Visa Reform Act, signed into law in May 2002, established the Student and Exchange Visitor Information System (SEVIS) to monitor information on foreign students and exchange visitors in the United States. The act required the Immigration and Naturalization Service (INS) to review academic institutions every two years to determine compliance with record keeping and reporting requirements. These requirements included reporting to the INS the failure of students to enroll within thirty days of being admitted into the United States, the current status of students, and their fields of study. SEVIS is an Internet system that enables schools and program sponsors to transmit information and electronic versions of school acceptance forms (I-20 and DS-2019) to DHS and the Department of State, which processes visas based on the approved school forms. It is administered within the Student and Exchange Visitor Program of the DHS Investigation and Customs Enforcement Bureau.

The concept of SEVIS and its basic structure are not new. Congress mandated that an electronic record system be established in 1996 as part of its review of the issues that contributed to the 1993 World Trade Center bombing. The system, called the Coordinated Interagency Partnership Regulating International Students (CIPRIS), was being developed by INS in collaboration with the Department State, United States Information Agency, Department of Education, and members of the educational and exchange program community. A pilot was launched, but CIPRIS was never fully implemented because Congress did not provide any funding (requiring that the system be completely user-paid) and because the education community voiced strenuous objections over ethical questions about its role in enforcing immigration law, particularly regarding the collection of fees.

In the aftermath of 9/11, academic leaders and organizations switched policies and endorsed the establishment of an electronic tracking system. The USA Patriot Act and the Enhanced Border Security and Visa Reform Act provided funding. Congress underscored the urgency of establishing the system by mandating compliance by 2003. INS launched SEVIS as a voluntary program on July 1, 2002, with mandatory participation for all institutions by January 30, 2003. Technical problems extended the deadline by two weeks. By August 1, 2003, information on all continuing foreign students and visitors was required to be updated into SEVIS in addition to the requirements for newly enrolled students and for those who changed status.

One year after the implementation of the program, government and school officials generally agree that SEVIS is a success. Initial complaints about difficult access and technical problems have largely been smoothed away. Some schools and recruiters have reported that SEVIS has made their work easier by reducing paper work. Electronic connectivity with DHS offices, ports of entry, federal offices, and embassies and consulates promises other efficiencies. Already, the ability for DHS to confirm student status through SEVIS has resulted in timelier processing of social security cards for legitimate students and scholars.

To ensure problems stay resolved, DHS organized a SEVIS Response Team. Operating at the National Records Center in Kansas City, the team responded on a 24-hour basis to calls for assistance from immigration inspectors at ports of entry, adjudicators, inspectors, schools, and students to resolve issues related to student admissions. A second team dedicated to customs and immigration inspectors at ports of entry assists in determining admission eligibility and proper SEVIS documentation.

Currently, 773,722 students and exchange visitors are registered in the system, representing many geographic origins (see figure 1). There are also 118,327 dependents of these people registered in SEVIS. The students and exchange visitors are enrolled in 7,288 SEVIS-registered schools, encompassing over 9,500 campuses (see figure 2).

The ability to quickly and accurately compile such information as well as to confirm the immigration and visa status of individual foreign students is a reasonable power for governments to have. It would be surprising (as

FIGURE 1. Geographic origins of students registered in SEVIS

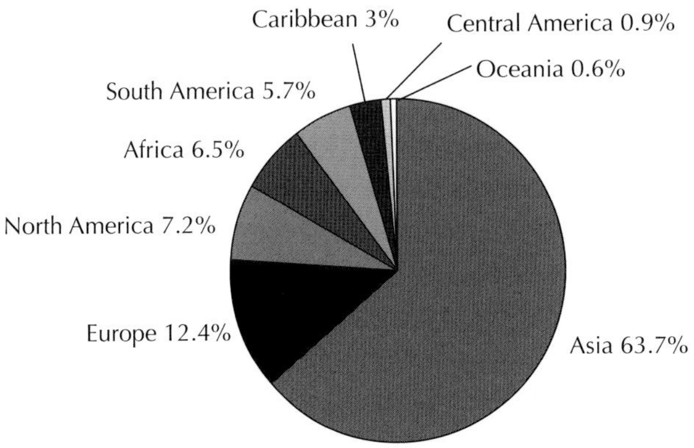

Caribbean 3%   Central America 0.9%
Oceania 0.6%
South America 5.7%
Africa 6.5%
North America 7.2%
Europe 12.4%
Asia 63.7%

Source: Department of Homeland Security data, 2004.

FIGURE 2. Top categories of SEVIS-certified schools

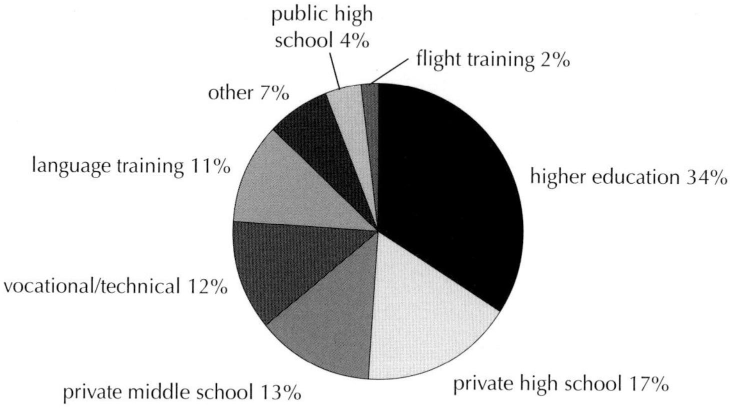

public high
school 4%

flight training 2%

other 7%

language training 11%

higher education 34%

vocational/technical 12%

private middle school 13%

private high school 17%

Source: Department of Homeland Security, 2004.

it was shocking to the Congress after 9/11) to think that a central authority did not have that ability from the beginning.

Moreover, few individuals in the visa and migration professions would disagree that the integrity of the paper-based system prior to SEVIS was questionable. A Justice Department internal review had recommended in March 2003 that SEVIS improve its procedures to detect fraud, but the system was able to spot about 3,000 student visa holders who did not report to classes, according to Undersecretary Asa Hutchinson in a May speech.[5] This was possible even though SEVIS did not include all the financial and other checks built into the CIPRIS version of the system.

Aside from the questions of integrity and security, it was apparent that the old paper-based system was inadequate to cope with the service needs of growing numbers of students or to efficiently assist the numerous institutions authorized to accept students. The number of foreign students in the United States grew from less than 155,000 in 1975 to 586,000 in 2003, but the paper-based system of registration and school certifications did not change significantly. A system to organize and manage information in a centralized computer database was needed to meet the needs of students and schools as well as the management requirements of INS and the consulates overseas long before the events of 9/11 demonstrated in stark relief the additional compelling security reasons.

Prior to 9/11, the academic community had argued that schools should not be party to enforcing immigration laws. This ethical position—more

---

5. Reported in Shane Harris, "Foreign Student Tracking System Called Inefficient, Intrusive," July 3, 2003, http://www.govexec.com/dailyfed/0703/070303h1.htm.

than the fee question which became prominent—prevented the predecessor to SEVIS from being implemented when CIPRIS was mandated in 1996. The events of 9/11 firmly settled the discussion. Without any doubt, all stakeholders—including school officials—have an interest in assuring that foreign students comply with American laws and regulations and that government has access to information by which it can identify people who might threaten the United States or abuse the knowledge and skills obtained from American schools and universities.

ALREADY, THE ABILITY FOR DHS TO CONFIRM STUDENT STATUS THROUGH SEVIS HAS RESULTED IN TIMELIER PROCESSING OF SOCIAL SECURITY CARDS FOR LEGITIMATE STUDENTS AND SCHOLARS.

In reality, the data collected by SEVIS is fairly basic. Much of it, if not all of it, is provided voluntarily by students in many different routine situations. Critical personal information is certainly provided to the federal government when students submit applications for visas at consulates and embassies overseas. It would be the height of naiveté to believe that government does not or should not evaluate the information for signs of threats to the homeland. The very process of obtaining a visa or legal status to study or conduct research in the United States is an action initiated knowingly by the students to allow law enforcement agencies to conduct security checks on them. It is reasonable to require students and schools where their enrollment determines their continuing legal status to update essential information over the several years a student typically stays in the United States.

As to the further question of proportionality, it is less an ethical issue than it is a calculation of practical measures and the balance of costs and benefits to the United States. The fulcrum to the balance is the point at which security measures become more burdensome and the added security too marginal weighted against the cost to administer the measures. Another consideration is the harm done to the benefits that unrestricted scholastic exchange provides for the homeland's long-term and immediate economic, political, and social health. Beneficial contributions include the $12 billion that foreign students inject into the American economy each year. Intangible benefits include nurturing democratic values and developing an appreciation and understanding of American life among foreign students, who in turn can affect political and social conditions in their own countries. Students expand the knowledge and appreciation of alternative cultures among the Americans with whom they live. Foreign talents and knowledge enrich American education programs. They contribute to the development of advanced American technology and its application.

There will always be a subjective element in any judgment of the balance, but I am persuaded to conclude SEVIS is both reasonable and proportional to American security needs. I believe many students and members of the education community would agree that SEVIS is no more than a modern and more efficient version of the visa, migration control, and security processes that have always been in place and that can be expected of any country accepting foreign students into its jurisdiction.

That being the case, SEVIS alone cannot explain the intense emotional concern over falling student enrollments and fears of restrictions on academic freedoms. Two other programs—NSEERS and IPASS—are keys to understanding how these impressions arose and to furthering this discussion on reasonable and proportional security measures.

NSEERS

Much of the criticisms of U.S. government attention to students and their visa programs is actually rooted in a program called NSEERS, the National Security Entry Exit Registration System. Strictly speaking, NSEERS is not a single system or law but refers to several policy decisions and regulations initiated by the Department of Justice through the INS in 2002 and 2003. The measures were designed to shore up perceived weaknesses in the immigration laws. Basically, the law enforcement community needed to know who was in the country, and the border control system in place could not provide this information quickly or accurately. Another objective, in the immediate aftermath of 9/11, was to devise a system that deterred other terrorists from entering the United States. NSEERS met these objectives by requiring certain visitors to the United States to undergo rigorous background checks. Because it was impossible to check all foreign

---

TOP FIVE COURSES OF STUDY BY ACTIVE STUDENTS

Business, Management, Marketing and
Related Support Services...............................19.8%
Engineering..14.3%
Computer and Information Sciences and
Support Services...9.4%
Basic Skills..5.4%
Liberal Arts and Sciences, General Studies
And Humanities...5.4%

Source: Department of Homeland Security, August 2004

visitors, priorities were set to target people from countries designated to be supporters of terrorism and from countries from where terrorists might be expected to emerge based on threat profiles gained from case experience.

The plan further sought to monitor people who traveled to the United States by requiring them to undergo secondary inspections upon arriving to the United States (including photographing and fingerprinting), to register their residence in the United States thirty days after entering the country and on an annual basis, and to depart the United States only after reporting to specific ports of exit. Failure to register or to report a departure properly was reason, under section 212(a)(3)(A)(ii) of the Immigration and Naturalization Act (INA), for denying a visa in a subsequent application or for refusing entry when the traveler returned to the United States. This section of the INA presumes the applicant is entering the United States to engage in unlawful activities, although the legal reasoning allowing for this section of law to apply in NSEERS cases was forced and established only after intense interagency debate. There were two general aspects to NSEERS—registration as visitors entered the United States, and a domestic registration for individuals residing in the United States, which was implemented in phases to cover an increasing number of nationalities.

NSEERS initially applied to male travelers ages 16 to 45 from Iran, Iraq, Libya, Sudan, and Syria. It then included male visitors from Pakistan, Saudi Arabia, and Yemen. From November 2002 to December 2003, a domestic registration phase required male citizens and nationals from these eight countries and seventeen others to register at INS (to become DHS) offices. There was an additional requirement to re-register on an annual basis. Of the twenty-five nationalities covered by NSEERS, all but North Korea were Arab or Islamic.

The design of a program targeted at specific nationality groups unsurprisingly led to criticisms of it being racially and religiously biased. The program drew further criticism for the unprepared manner in which its registration and re-registration requirements were implemented, which, judging from the stream of press reports, was chaotic, inefficient, and confusing. Confusion was also a characteristic of the departure requirements to the degree that travelers who wanted to comply could not locate inspectors to perform the function. The number of airports and land ports designated to receive and particularly send off travelers was limited, which served to create an image of American insensitivity to the inconveniences NSEERS caused to national and religious groups and bred the impression of retributive vindictiveness being unfairly applied to the group for the actions of individuals. In reality, INS (DHS) was conscientiously responsive to these concerns. It greatly expanded the number of ports and made instructions clearer and more accessible through outreach and different media. But damage had been done, and it continues with each singling out of an NSEERS-affected visitor upon arrival and departure.

Examples of the negative impact included: Loss revenue for health care and tourism industries; inflexible application (as seen in the example of an Australian defense force officer of Iraqi heritage transiting Florida and being stopped); outraged commentary in Indonesian and Malaysian press; and continuous complaints from foreign embassies about the treatment meted out to its diplomats and dignitaries. The ambassador from Bangladesh strongly protested his country's inclusion into NSEERS. Reports from the U.S. embassy in Dhaka cited examples of students of good academic standing and background denied entry or held for up to fifteen hours at airports upon their arrival in the United States during summer breaks. Because of their longer stays in the United States, foreign students and exchange visitors make up the larger percentage of the NSEERS registrants. Many of them have expressed a sense of humiliation when singled out for special security scrutiny and for fingerprinting, associated in many minds with criminality. There is little doubt that the implementation of NSEERS has contributed to the decline in foreign students and has created negative impressions among the very people the United States needs to convert to ideals of Western democracy, rule of law, and social equality.

Under shadows of criticism and concern from the consequences NSEERS, DHS assumed responsibility for the program from the Department of Justice. DHS began anew the interagency discussion on the value of the program. The domestic registration phase was declared over and re-registration requirements were suspended in December 2003. Students registered in SEVIS were no longer required to register and re-register under NSEERS. However, it was impossible to obtain interagency consensus to dismantle the policy on the entry and departure of the original eight Arab and Islamic countries.

The underlying motive for NSEERS—which is that security of a nation requires a border system that registers foreign entries and departures—is reasonable. It is difficult to think of any country that does not have an entry and exit inspection, but the United States has not had an exit inspection process for decades. Instead, it relies on airlines and travelers to self-report their departure by depositing their immigration card (form I-94) with INS. INS staff then enters the data from accumulated cards at a later time to record departures into the INS central database. The system is haphazard and contributes to the uncertainty of who is in the country at any particular time. The solution is to establish a comprehensive entry/exit system.

This is the purpose of US-VISIT, or United States Visitor and Immigrant Status Indicator Technology. Like SEVIS, the concept was not new and its development was underway in 1996. And, like SEVIS, 9/11 gave the program greater urgency. Established in 2003, US-VISIT has been incrementally implemented under firm Congressionally mandated dates. The 9/11 Commission report cited its value and continuing success in establishing an electronic (and biometrically supported) system to record all travelers. Once fully in place, NSEERS will become redundant, but until US-VISIT is fully operational, the loophole in knowledge about foreign visitors within our borders must be plugged by the continuation of NSEERS.

The balance sheet on the proportionality test of NSEERS, however, is preponderantly negative. There has been no evidence of any terrorist caught because of NSEERS. Neither the Federal Bureau of Investigations nor Immigration and Customs Enforcement could explain satisfactorily the value of the information they collected and why it needs to be collected in the visibly offensive way that it is. The fact is that the data sought by NSEERS is mostly obtainable from the routine processes of vetting visa applications through consulates and embassies. Following the recommendation of the 9/11 Commission to justify the continuation of security measures by how they materially add to homeland security, the reasonable justification of the establishment of NSEERS is outweighed by its failure to meet the proportional test.

However, neither NSEERS alone nor the combination of NSEERS and SEVIS adequately explains the volume of complaints about government scrutiny of students. Most of the students affected by post-9/11 concerns over terrorists are from India and China. Students from Asia account for 64 percent of the approximately 770,000 students and exchange visitors in the United States. The Council of Graduate Schools, according to the American Association for Advancement of Science, reported that applications for graduate studies in 2004 from China declined by 76 percent compared with 2003 figures, and those from India by 58 percent.

India and China are not notable as hotbeds of international terrorism. They are not mentioned in NSEERS at all in any of its nationality criteria in any of its phases. The issue here is about technology transfer and how procedures established for the Cold War against the Soviet Union and China were intensified by the concerns over terrorism from the Middle East.

IPASS

In October 2001, President Bush issued Presidential Directive HSPD 2, which mandated the creation of measures to combat terrorism by prohibiting certain foreign students from "receiving education and training in sensitive areas, including areas of study with direct application to the development and use of weapons of mass destruction." The impetus for the directive is easy to understand. As Congressman Ralph Hall of Texas at hearings in October 2002 on the status of the directive commented, "We must be sure that we don't help train the enemy. We did just that for the 9/11 cowards by allowing them to go to flight schools. If we do that again with biological and chemical agents, the price would be unthinkable."[6]

In a briefing to members of the higher education community, Presidential Science Advisor John Marburger outlined the Administration's plans to address the issue. The key feature was the establishment of the Interagency Panel on Advanced Science Security (IPASS). The panel would review visa applications referred to it by the State Department and the INS (now DHS) and make recommendations to the consular and INS officers who adjudicated the application for visa or student status. It was estimated that IPASS would screen 1,000–2,000 visa applications a year (out of an estimated 175,000 new students and scholars entering the country per year). The panel would consider such factors as the student's country of origin and area of study, with particular emphasis on whether the studies involve advanced programs in sensitive subjects that are uniquely available in the United States.

Although details and a written version of the plans are not yet available, most educators, including the Association of American Universities, believed the establishment of IPASS to be a positive step. As observed by one Vanderbilt University commentator in a policy and opinion piece, universities liked the plan's emphasis on stopping people before they entered the United States, as opposed to attempting to prevent students already studying here from accessing sensitive material, or, worse, enduring a government review of course offerings.[7]

As of today, however, IPASS has not been implemented. In the meantime, its objective to control access to sensitive knowledge and training is being partially met by existing Department of State measures under its Visa Mantis program. This program requires consular officers to request a Washington clearance before visas are issued to students or visitors who may come into access with technologies that have dual military and civilian use. Technological fields are listed in a Technology Alert List (TAL) and vary by

6. House of Representatives Science Committee hearings, October 10, 2002, quoted in Harvey Black, "Foreign Student Scrutiny," *The Scientist*, online daily news, October 21, 2002, http://www.biomedcentral.com/news/20021021/06/.

7. Jeff Vincent, "Access by Foreign Students to Sensitive Areas of Study," *Exploration*, online research journal of Vanderbilt University, July 18, 2002, http://www.vanderbilt.edu/exploration/policy/dcreports.php?DcreportID=3.

country. TAL and Visa Mantis mostly apply to countries opposed to the United States during the Cold War.

Over the years, the TAL has been streamlined to reflect improving political relationships (especially with China), the growth of international commerce, and the realities that technology is no longer restricted to Western countries, let alone to the United States.   Strict application of TAL was in some instances becoming a barrier to efficient commerce and academic exchanges of benefit to both sides.   Until 9/11, the trend was to match the political and commercial reality by making Visa Mantis more routine and by refining, if not reducing, the list of fields included on the TAL.   The cases that continued to be submitted were screened quickly in Washington, and it was possible to establish an interagency agreement to fix processing timelines that allowed visa officers to issue visas if there were no negative replies within two weeks of initiating requests for security checks.

After 9/11, visa officers became more cautious and the policy of the State Department emphasized the security aspects of the visa processes, which included greater adherence to Visa Mantis considerations. Additionally, Visa Condor was established in 2002 as a parallel program to NSEERS.   Although Visa Condor was more selectively applied based on travel and background criteria compared with how INS implemented NSEERS, it added yet another directive to field officers to tighten the security procedures for all visa applicants.   The consequence was a flood of requests for security checks that overwhelmed the Washington interagency process to ensure proper checks were completed within the previously agreed timelines.   The backlog in 2003 grew from 14,000 cases to 25,000. The reorganization of INS into four distinct units in DHS and one at Department of Justice compounded delays as office responsibilities and procedures were realigned.

In the meantime, the Department of State responded to the processing delays, and the disruptions caused by the Visa Mantis procedures began to smooth over.   Although reestablishing fixed timeframes remains elusive, today almost all requests for security clearances are completed within thirty days of their submission, and this has become an unofficial goal for Consular Affairs.   Moreover, the Washington interagency process continues to improve its efficiency through automation and better interoperability among agencies. For Chinese exchange students, there are additional efforts to address problems caused by the short validity of visas issued them, which requires students to renew their visas more frequently than other nationals. Each application, in turn, required another security check.   Recognizing this problem, the length of the validity of a Visa Mantis clearance was extended so that requests for security checks for the same student for the same program did not have to be repeated in subsequent visa applications. Another proposal is to pre-clear students returning home during school breaks to minimize the time needed to receive a visa once an application is submitted.

With attention to addressing issues and improving the procedures causing delays, and until IPASS can be established, it is reasonable to continue the security processes already in place. The proportional consideration and how much the Visa Mantis process contributes to the war on terrorism remain unanswered questions. In this regard, it is relevant to note that public discussions on IPASS predicted that the number of students affected will not be large. According to a Georgia State University Economics Professor, using National Science Foundation data, U.S. universities awarded 62,000 doctorates in the 1960s to students with visas, 1,215 of whom were from Iran, Iraq, Libya, Sudan, and Syria—NSEERS countries. Of those degrees, only 147 were conferred in sensitive research areas. The Department of State issued 619,475 visas issued to students and exchange visitors in FY 2001. Of that number, 15,384 were issued to nationals from the eight NSEERS countries, of which about 11,000 came from two countries: Saudi Arabia and Pakistan.[8] This number includes dependents, making the total number of students and exchange visitors actually handling sensitive information smaller. On the other hand, as noted, the largest number of students affected by the more intense scrutiny on controlling sensitive technology and skills to create weapons of mass destruction from foreign terrorists are Chinese and Indian, as well as Russian.

As we consider SEVIS, NSEERS, IPASS, and any other measure we devise to protect our homeland, we want to be sure of our objectives and that we are not applying criteria established for oranges when we really want to select apples. The stakes are high. In congressional testimony, University of California Santa Cruz Chancellor M.R.C. Greenwood said the United States is "no longer the only nation that can provide access to specialized information …We would be much better advised to strengthen our overall science and technology enterprise than to restrict access."[9]

For the foreseeable future as the terrorist threat looms, U.S. visa policy and procedures will continue to be in flux. Today, the challenge for the United States in international trade is balancing the security needs with the free flow of goods. Regarding international academic exchanges, the

---

8. U.S. Department of State Bureau of Consulate Affairs, *Report of the Visa Office 2001*, Department of State publication 11073, Washington, DC, August 2003.

9. House of Representatives Science Committee hearings, October 10, 2002, quoted in Harvey Black, "Foreign Student Scrutiny," *The Scientist,* http://www.biomedcentral.com/news/20021021/06/.

challenge is similar: balancing the desire and need for a more internationally diverse student pool while seeking to vigorously review the entry and exit of people across our borders. Plainly, 9/11 changed the world and the ways we did business, conducted diplomacy, and secured our borders. It is safe to predict that SEVIS, NSEERS, and IPASS will undergo continuous retooling to make them more secure, efficient, and less burdensome.

10. Wireless File to Web: State Department's Print and Electronic Media in the Arab World

Howard Cincotta

An alien political scientist trying to plumb the mysteries of U.S. foreign policy might well be transfixed by a daily ritual that most citizens find less than riveting: the noon briefing at the Department of State ("noon" being an approximation of when the briefing actually takes place). Our alien researcher would be struck, one suspects, less by the careful, incantatory nature of the Department's responses than by the expectation that the United States has views on virtually every event, consequential or not, occurring anywhere in the world. ("The U.S. looks forward to continued dialogue"... "The U.S. applauds"... "supports"... "is gratified" ... "views with alarm" ... "offers condolences"... "is monitoring the situation closely" ... "will consult with its friends and allies...") It can all add up to a lot of words.

On a typical Washington workday, American officials from the president to assistant secretaries and press officers issue a remarkable mélange of remarks, speeches, press releases, clarifications, op-eds, fact sheets, white papers, and briefings relevant to foreign policy, whether the interest level is general (Iraqi political developments), specialized (the fate of Pacific salmon), or arcane (museum management in Azerbaijan). The numbers vary, but on an average day, State's Bureau of International Information Programs (IIP) moves between fifteen and twenty-five such texts, transcripts, and other documents emanating from the agencies of the foreign affairs community.

Wherever their origins, these documents constitute the daily grist of foreign policy materials that the State Department's foreign service officers, writers, editors, translators, graphic designers, and technology professionals must assess, edit, format, translate, illustrate, and transmit to embassies and foreign publics throughout the world.

Although their value as news may be clear, it is unlikely that these activities contribute much to changing foreign attitudes toward American policies, especially in the Arab and Muslim worlds. On the other hand, if the spigot of these public diplomacy materials were shut down or reduced significantly, the silence would be deafening.

The challenge remains: how to penetrate this constant white noise of diplomacy and reach vital new international audiences by changing the subject and nature of the diplomatic discourse.

The File

The starting point for assessing the State Department's output of public diplomacy materials—print and electronic—is the daily Washington File of texts and transcripts that are edited and posted on the Web site of the Bureau of International Information Programs and transmitted in five regional editions to U.S. embassies and missions around the world. Substantial portions are also translated into six languages: Arabic, Spanish, French, Russian, Farsi, and Chinese. In turn, embassies around the world can opt for providing direct links to the Washington File, or they can repackage, "brand," and retransmit the File's stream of official statements and remarks through their own distribution channels. Most embassies, in fact, do both.

IIP itself is the product of two significant reorganizations of the Clinton Administration: an internal reinvention exercise, and the merger of the U.S. Information Agency (USIA) with the State Department.

In 1994, USIA's Information Bureau, designated as a "reinvention laboratory," created a set of multi-functional "thematic" and "geographic" teams that combined Washington File and other writer-editors with program officers who managed traveling speaker programs and other information resource specialists, graphic artists, Webmasters, and, increasingly, technology and network specialists.

Team-based reinvention may have had the most direct effect on day-to-day operations of IIP, but the biggest psychological impact came with the 1999 consolidation of USIA and the Department of State. In reality, consolidation was a euphemism. Professional courtesies and respect aside, the logic of bureaucracies is ineluctable: large entities swallow up smaller ones, and the State Department was no exception.

Under consolidation, the U.S. Information Agency was eliminated; the Bureau of Educational and Cultural Affairs moved to State relatively unscathed; and USIA's Bureau of Information, shorn of some functions, became State's Office of International Information Programs.   USIA's regional offices, composed largely of foreign service officers, became public diplomacy units within the traditional regional bureaus of the State Department. The Voice of America (VOA) moved to a new agency, the

International Broadcasting Bureau (IBB), supervised by an independent board of governors. The IBB now comprises a mix of old and new broadcasting endeavors: VOA, Radio Sawa (Arabic), Radio Farda (Farsi), Radio Free Europe, Radio Free Asia, and Radio/TV Martí (broadcasting to Cuba).

Although State's Office of International Information Programs was later upgraded to a bureau, its head, designated as a "coordinator," has been unable to achieve assistant secretary status. The State Department created a new senior position, undersecretary for public diplomacy and public affairs, to oversee the two former USIA bureaus—International Information Programs and Educational and Cultural Affairs—as well as State's own Bureau of Public Affairs (which was never part of USIA).

Although reorganizations and technology have transformed the Washington File over the years, in many ways the File remains remarkably close to its 1935 inception as a series of radio-teletype bulletins subsequently know as the Wireless File (a name it retained until the 1990s). In fact, the Wireless/Washington File can lay legitimate claim to being America's most venerable public diplomacy program, predating formation of the U.S. Information Agency (1953), Voice of America (1942), and the first government-sponsored cultural exchange programs, which can probably be dated to a 1936 Pan American conference in Buenos Aires.

The Wireless File had its origins in the complaint of a Roosevelt Administration ambassador who found the State Department's cables about as informative and current "as a Roman ruin." In many ways, the mission of today's Internet-era Washington File has changed remarkably little: the packaging and transmitting of authoritative texts, transcripts, and other policy-related materials in a timely fashion. (Although superficially resembling a wire service, the Washington File is not a news outlet and neither covers breaking news nor competes with operations like the Associated Press or Reuters.)

For more than sixty years, the Wireless/Washington File compiled official texts for exclusive delivery to U.S. embassies and missions worldwide. For the past decade, it has published them on the Web, as well. When embassies have been asked to evaluate Washington's information products, the File has consistently been rated first. (Cultural exchanges constitute a different program category.) By providing the authoritative policy framework within which every foreign service officer dealing with public affairs can operate, there is little doubt that the File would receive the same ranking in such a survey today.

The Arabic edition of the Washington/Wireless File began in 1977. As with the other language editions of the File, translation capacity remains the chief constraint on its capacity to move Arabic versions of the steady torrent of policy materials issuing from Washington. Add the complex and polarizing dimensions of the Israeli-Palestinian conflict, the global war on terrorism, and military campaigns in Afghanistan and Iraq, and you have a small office that has operated under extraordinary duress not just since 9/11, but since the 1991 Gulf War, followed by Bosnian and Kosovo crises of the late 1990s.

The number of writer/editors for the regional English and Arabic edition of the File has not grown in the dramatic fashion that one might expect in the aftermath of 9/11 and the furor over public perceptions of the United States in the Arab world. Despite the post-9/11 mandate for public diplomacy that operates "wider, deeper, and younger" than previously, staff and resource increases have been modest at best. Today there are eight full-time writer/editors, including five Arabic-language editors, responsible for Middle Eastern/North African and South Asian editions of the Washington File. They, along with other information specialists and Arabic-language Webmasters, also oversee a large number of Web pages and online document collections.

Nevertheless, the IIP Middle East staff has managed to increase its output of Arabic-language texts substantially, from an average of 3,000 to more than 10,000 words a day, primarily through the use of an expanded network of contract translators in Washington and overseas. File editors constantly look for feature items and other kinds of articles to lighten the daily load of policy pronouncements and offer subjects that present images of America outside the narrow prism of foreign policy and military operations.

Editors have also become adept at the practice of offering exclusives to major Arabic news outlets for translated versions of op-eds by senior officials, notably the secretary of state. Outside of television and radio broadcasting, such high-level op-ed placements are one of the most reliable means of placing an unmediated statement of U.S. policy before a mass Arab readership today.

Web Sites and E-Mail Publishing

IIP's predecessor, the U.S. Information Agency, was an early adopter of Internet technology, and USIA had a Web site carrying Washington File texts online by 1995. Less visible but perhaps more important, USIA's first Webmasters leveraged the growing popularity of e-mail to design simple, automated processes to permit the hosting of overseas embassy and U.S. Information Service (USIS) Web sites. Many of those early USIS sites may have had more symbolic than program value, but they introduced a generation of public diplomacy officers to the promise and perils of Web work—and helped lay the foundation for today's extensive network of overseas embassy, consulate, and mission Web sites.[1]

The Washington File and IIP Web sites are all easily accessible through Internet search engines; however, users will not find links to them through the main State Department site.[2] The reason: the 1953 legislation establishing the former U.S. Information Agency, the Smith-Mundt Act, prohibits the "dissemination" to American audiences of public diplomacy information intended for foreign audiences. As a result, IIP's Internet addresses are widely advertised overseas but not published or promoted openly in the United States. (IIP is not to be confused with State's Bureau of Public Affairs, which does have a mandate of communicating with the American public and manages the main Web site.)

The Internet transformed the File from a narrowly focused, embassy-only operation into a public Web product. The transition has been slow and in some respects remains incomplete. Nevertheless, users of State's IIP Web site can find current, authoritative packages of U.S. policy materials on a wide range of subjects—from biotechnology to Middle East affairs—presented as collections of texts or formatted as special Web pages. Many are available in Arabic, French, and other languages, and feature links to other online information resources.

Take a snapshot of IIP's Web site in the summer of 2004 and you would find Web pages and online document collections devoted to Iraq, Afghanistan, the Middle East Peace Process, the assistance program known as the Middle East Partnership Initiative, U.S.–Middle East Free Trade Area, the work of the nongovernmental youth initiative Seeds of Peace, as well as more broadly focused pages devoted to the war on terrorism, war crimes tribunals, and building democracy around the world. Also appearing are an online photo gallery depicting Iraq's transition to sovereignty in June and July 2004 and the humanitarian response to a major February earthquake in Morocco. IIP maintains a Web page in Farsi for Iranian audiences, as well.

Overall, the IIP Web site averages roughly 70,000 page views a day—a figure that will spike during a period of conflict or intense focus on international events. When the Abu Ghraib prison scandal broke in April 2004, for example, activity increased 14 percent on the entire IIP Web site and 30 percent for its Arabic-language sections.

According to a recent congressional statement by Patricia Harrison, assistant secretary for educational and cultural affairs, 470 other Arabic

---

1. These sites are linked to http://usembassy.state.gov.

2. http://www.state.gov.

Web sites now link to IIP's main Middle East Web page.[3] She also reported that analysis indicates that 85 percent of IIP's Web users are based overseas, with more than 50 percent of that number from the Middle East, notably Saudi Arabia, Egypt, United Arab Emirates, Kuwait, and Syria.

Moreover, IIP has maintained focus on e-mail as the genuine "killer app" of the Internet era: ubiquitous, familiar, and available in locations with only the most tenuous electronic connections. Among the options open to users of the IIP's Web site: e-mail delivery of policy materials using Listserv. In English, for example, recipients can sign up for the daily Washington File in English or Arabic, or for selected materials relating only to Middle East policy or Iraq. Roughly 1,200 subscribers currently receive the Arabic edition of the Washington File by e-mail.

IIP recently began offering another option: automatic streaming of Washington File headline stories to a user's own Web site or Internet news reader using an application called RSS (Real Simple Syndication). By pasting in a small block of code, users can choose from such automated feeds as Washington File Top Stories or Middle East and North Africa Top Stories. IIP Webmasters anticipate that RSS will becomes a standard way of highlighting up-to-date policy statements on embassy Web pages.

Lost in Translation

In contrast to the Washington File's continuity, the history of print publications and books in English and Arabic is much more diffuse. Like USIA before it, IIP maintains a publications office that produces books, pamphlets, reports, posters, small traveling exhibits known as paper shows, and other materials on current topics such as human rights, biodiversity, HIV/AIDS, trade, Iraq, and the 2004 elections. In addition, the publications office maintains a list of so-called Basic Publications intended to provide fundamental information about the United States, its society and values. Titles encompass the *Outline* book series on American history, economy, geography, and literature, guides for foreign students planning to study in the United States, and publications on the news media, environment, culture, an annotated and illustrated edition of the U.S. Constitution, and other topics.

Except for titles that are region-specific (NATO, Western Hemisphere affairs), virtually all of these publications are translated into Arabic. They are free, attractively designed, usually illustrated, and written to appeal to a broad international audience educated at a roughly secondary-school level.

---

3. Harrison is currently the acting undersecretary for public diplomacy and public affairs, as well.

The discouraging news is that production and distribution have changed little in the last forty years. Embassies receive printing allocations as part of their annual budget and order special and basic publications from those accounts throughout the year. This may well be a sensible and businesslike method of filling an embassy's publications needs for free distribution to foreign audiences. With many competing responsibilities, however, embassies have neither the staff nor the funds to explore innovative ways of distributing publications to reach wider audiences otherwise untouched by official U.S. government programming.

During FY 2003, for example, the Cairo embassy ordered only 6,300 publications in total; Rabat ordered 6,000, and the United Arab Emirates 4,500. Three posts in India (New Delhi, Chennai, Mumbai) ordered fewer than 14,000 in total; Islamabad, 7,200. These numbers are dwarfed by the population and strategic importance of these countries. Moreover, they do not begin to meet any reasonable projection of the key audiences of students, officials, opinion leaders—the so-called "successor generations"— who might well be eager to receive such information.

In the 1960s and 1970s, when overseas magazines and publications flourished, USIA operated full-service printing plants in Beirut, Mexico City, and Manila, along with a smaller facility in Vienna that principally served eastern Europe and the Soviet Union. Beirut shut down during Lebanon's civil war in 1976, and the Mexico City plant never recovered from a devastating earthquake in 1985.

The State Department's largest printing facility, Manila, possesses high capacity, operates cost effectively, employs the latest digital technology, and manipulates global shipping networks with great skill. Its fundamental problem is geographic: posts outside East Asia face the unenviable choice of rapid but expensive air shipment, or cheaper but slower delivery by sea freight. Only larger embassies have the resources to opt for local commercial printing. So far, the State Department has been unable to develop and implement a comprehensive plan for exploiting new digital, "just-in-time" technologies at smaller, scattered facilities for fast and flexible distribution of printed materials worldwide.

The Internet, fortunately, has erased many of the distinctions between print and electronic publication, and most IIP titles—old or new—are available online in English and foreign languages.

Booked Up

The U.S. embassy in Cairo has been home to an Arabic-language book translation and distribution program since the 1950s. An arrangement with a Jordanian publisher in the mid-1980s has evolved into a similar but smaller program operated out of the Amman embassy. Other government agencies, notably the U.S. Agency for International Development (USAID), and private organizations operate Arabic book programs in Cairo, as well.

Today, the Arabic Book Program in Cairo and Amman, with a modest annual budget of $50,000 and only two full-time local staffers, subsidizes the translation and production of approximately twelve titles a year through a lengthy process of consultation, selection, and production. First, the Regional Book Office in Cairo asks local publishers as well as other Arabic-speaking posts to suggest titles of interest to them. Next, an embassy committee consisting of Americans as well as local staff meet to select the books for translation for the year. The criteria include embassy and regional program priorities as well as broader American studies topics. Copyright clearances, which can be time consuming, are generally provided by IIP in Washington.

The topics are quite eclectic: from heavy-duty tomes on international affairs and American society (*Honey and Vinegar: Incentives, Sanctions, and Foreign Policy*, edited by Richard W. Haass and Meghan L. O'Sullivan; *Deadly Struggle For Middle East Peace*, by Geoffrey Kemp and Jeremy Pressman; *Community Works: The Revival of Civil Society in America*, by E. J. Dionne) to fiction and history (*Cold Mountain*, by Charles Frazier; and *Abraham Lincoln and the Second American Revolution*, by James M. McPherson).

Contemporary titles on economics and business management are well represented, along with literary classics such as *The Federalist Papers*, DeToqueville's *Democracy in America*, and *The Adventures of Huckleberry Finn* (the latter surely being a challenging task from English to Arabic).

In 2003, the book program received an additional $50,000 to publish a series of nine young adult titles that featured such Newberry Award-winners as *Sounder*, by William Armstrong; *The Summer of the Swans*, by Betsy Byars; and *The Greatest: Mohammed Ali*, by Walter Dean Myers. Madeline L'Engle's fantasy classic, *A Wrinkle in Time*, is in production. Unfortunately, the one-time funding was not renewed, and the embassy is not planning any further young adult translations.

Typical print runs are 3,000 copies, of which the embassy buys back 1,000 for local programs and distribution to embassies throughout the region. The remaining 2,000 are sold by publishers locally. According to the Cairo embassy, relatively few copies are distributed commercially outside Egypt.

In the words of the 2003 report of the U.S. Advisory Group on Public Diplomacy for the Arab and Muslim World, chaired by former ambassador Edward P. Djerejian:

> Book translation programs...have been small in scope, focused more on popular volumes related to the United States and are limited in distribution. Still, they appear to have been largely successful. Importantly, the costs of translation of each book (less than $5,000 on the average) are strikingly reasonable when one considers the benefits of the translation.[4]

The report goes on to recommend a huge increase in book translation through an American Knowledge Library Initiative that would underwrite as many as 1000 translated books annually—a quantum leap not only in titles but in potential readership.

USAID Egypt has undertaken a new Arabic distribution initiative under the Administration's Middle East Partnership Initiative. Although lacking a translation component, USAID has selected translated and original Arabic-language books, and packaged 3,000 sets in shelf units for presentations to fourth- and fifth-grade classrooms in Alexandria. USAID is also developing children's titles under the "Alam Simsim" (Egyptian Sesame Street) program. Outside government, Scholastic Publishing has a project called "Maktabati al Arabiyya" (My Arabic Library).

Individually, each of these disparate publishing initiatives—IIP publications (print and electronic), overseas printing operations, and Arabic-language book publishing—support critically important public affairs objectives. It is equally clear, however, that none of them has broken out of the paradigm of producing printed information for relatively small target audiences that are deemed to be opinion leaders or otherwise influential within their community, profession, or country. Certainly none of these programs has yet been integrated into any kind of overarching vision for public diplomacy in the Middle East, or elsewhere in the world for that matter.

Magazine World

General-interest magazines for foreign readers, once a mainstay of public diplomacy, have lately made a modest comeback after most were eliminated in the mid-1990s.

USIA published an Arabic-language magazine for the Middle East and North Africa from the late 1950s until the Six Day War in June 1967. Later that year, USIA launched a feature magazine for sub-Saharan Africa in English and French called *Topic*, along with a separate Arabic edition

---

4. Edward P. Djerejian, *Changing Minds, Winning Peace: A New Strategic Direction for U.S. Public Diplomacy in the Arab and Muslim World*, report of the U.S. Advisory Group on Public Diplomacy for the Arab and Muslim World (Washington, DC: 2003), 40.

named *al Majal*. In 1971, *al Majal* became an independent magazine with its own editorial staff.

Al Majal joined a family of magazines: a worldwide intellectual and cultural quarterly, *Dialogue*, with multiple languages, including Arabic, and what was in many ways the agency's flagship periodical—the monthly Russian-language magazine for the Soviet Union, *America Illustrated*. (USIA published more specialized journals as well: *Economic Impact*, *Problems of Communism*, and *English Teaching Forum*.)

Although magazine content and approach were as varied as the audience, all the magazines shared certain common denominators. Most usually featured a mix of commissioned, staff-written, and reprint articles (*Dialogue* consisted substantially of reprints from commercial and intellectual American magazines). All maintained a tradition of graphic excellence, with heavy reliance on photographs. Embassies ordered magazines like *al Majal*, *Topic*, and *Dialogue* from the Manila, Vienna, and other printing facilities. They were not sold or distributed commercially. The one exception, *America Illustrated*, was sold through kiosks as part of a cultural exchange agreement with the Soviet Union. (An attempt to sell ads in the magazines after the Gulf War in 1991 ended in failure.)

Al Majal, whose editorial offices moved from Washington to Tunis and eventually back to Washington, ceased operations along with USIA's other magazines in 1994 under budget pressures and a reorganization that was part of Vice President Gore's government reinvention initiative. There was another, internal factor. With the demise of the Soviet Union, it was no longer possible to justify publication of a lavish, picture-oriented magazine like *America Illustrated* when Western publications and books were flooding into Russia and Central Asia. Like chains linked to an anchor, once USIA threw *America Illustrated* over the side, it dragged all the other magazines overboard as well.

USIA's first venture back into the world of periodicals was an innovative effort in 1996 to leverage the emerging Internet technology through a series of electronic journals that would reflect five broad subject areas: foreign policy, economics, democracy and human rights, global issues such as environment and drug trafficking, and U.S. society and values. In sharp contrast to the old feature magazines, electronic journals are conceived of explicitly as packages of policy materials—from official and non-governmental sources—coupled with bibliographies, Internet sites, and listings of information resources. The topic selection involves not only consultations among IIP offices and State regional and functional bureaus, but input from an advisory panel of representatives from twenty-four overseas posts.

The journals, all now branded as *eJournal* and featured prominently on the IIP Web site, are produced in Arabic, English, French, Spanish, Portuguese, and Russian. They can be accessed three ways: in plain text, HTML, or formatted (PDF) versions. Embassies and other journal recipients also have the option of downloading complete issues or selecting individual articles. In a recent survey, more than 70 percent of posts found the electronic journals "highly" relevant to their public diplomacy programs and close to half said that they printed entire journals for distribution to selected audiences.

A rundown of IIP's recent *eJournal* articles gives a sense of their range: *Foreign Policy Agenda*: "U.S. and NATO: An Alliance of Purpose"; *Economic Perspectives*: "Challenges to Energy Security"; *Issues of Democracy*: "Access to the Courts: Equal Justice for All"; *Global Issues*: "Shared Oceans, Shared Future"; and *Society and Values*: "Americans at the Table: Reflections on Food and Culture."

One notable fact about electronic journals is that, unlike most of IIP Web pages, articles do not use materials that originate from the Washington File. Journal articles are either commissioned, reprinted from other U.S. publications, or written by IIP or other State Department staff.

The April 2004 issue of *Global Issues*, "Shared Oceans, Shared Future," is typical in its balance. It contains "Diplomacy and the Oceans," by the State Department's David Balton, deputy assistant secretary for oceans and fisheries; an interview with noted oceanographer Robert Ballard, discoverer of the *Titanic*; and commentary by independent authorities ("Communities Around the World Protect the Underwater World," by Brian Huse, executive director of the Coral Reef Alliance).

The strengths and limitations of electronic journals derive from their Internet origin. As electronic documents, users have unprecedented flexibility in how they can manipulate, format, excerpt, and reproduce the journals in their entirety, or just retrieve specific articles. But Internet delivery also means that costs in time and materials for local reproduction and distribution land on the users, not the publishers. Embassies, for example, have neither staff nor resources to download, print, and distribute substantial numbers of journal copies to new or expanded readers who otherwise lack reliable Internet connections through which they individually could view electronic journals.

Hi Magazine

One new publication has broken out of old distribution models to reach potentially new and critically important audiences in the Middle East: the new Arabic-language youth magazine, *Hi*. Launched in July 2003, *Hi* is a glossy, 72-page Arabic monthly that targets 18- to 35-year-old Arabs with articles on education, technology, careers, health, culture, lifestyles, relationships, music, film, entertainment—in other words the kind of interests held in common by young people around the world who, if not middle-class and affluent, aspire to be. The primary topics missing from *Hi*'s list of interests: foreign policy and politics.

Although *Hi* receives funding and editorial oversight from IIP, it is edited by the commercial Magazine Group in Washington; printed at State's Manila facility; distributed through the Levant Group in London, Paris, and Beirut; and backed by a modest advertising and promotion budget handled by the advertising firm Saatchi & Saatchi.

Hi prints almost 45,000 copies per month, which are sold in eighteen countries, along with copies distributed through the American embassies. The magazine remains blocked from distribution in three critically important countries: Saudi Arabia, Syria, and Algeria.

Hi maintains two Web sites: the Arabic-language www.himag.com and an abridged English-language site, www.hiinternational.com. Despite the fact that the magazine is currently unavailable in their country, Saudis appear to be among the most frequent visitors to *Hi*'s Web site.

The evidence for *Hi*'s success is mixed, and depends in large part on what criteria one uses. On one hand, *Hi* has had difficulty selling its newsstand copies and has recently dropped its price twice to make it more affordable; it now sells for the equivalent of $.70 to $1.00 per copy. This is hardly an unexpected hurdle in the highly competitive commercial magazine world, however—nor when considering *Hi*'s launch during the build-up to war in Iraq and continuing Israeli-Palestinian violence.

Despite initial skepticism from readers because *Hi* is an American-sponsored periodical, the early evidence suggests that it is succeeding in reaching a younger Arabic audience with a formula of useful, entertaining, and interactive features. Moreover, the fact that the magazine's sales have continued to rise at a time when polls indicate unprecedented negative views of America in the Arab world would appear to be an indicator that it is finding and connecting with new audiences.

Hi recently launched special promotions in Tunisia and Kuwait, for example, and while sales figures are pending, the editors have noted an increase in letters from both countries. (The promotion includes distribution through Starbucks outlets in Kuwait.)

Sajed al Abdalli, a well-known Kuwaiti commentator who is frequently highly critical of the United States, recently described picking up a copy of *Hi* at Starbucks and finding it "an eloquent Arabic language magazine aimed at youth, printed in the latest style, produced professionally...and in sync with its readers."

A Web site survey conducted on *Hi*'s first anniversary, while informal and self-selecting, found that a majority rated the magazine useful and informative; perhaps most significant, more than 40 percent of respondents said the magazine had changed their views of America for the better.

Interactivity appears to be an important element in *Hi*'s appeal. Every issue carries some sort of contest; articles provide links, sidebars, advice, and additional sources of information. Equally important, every issue carries a series of Questions to America/Questions from America, which are often forwarded to academic or other experts for answers. *Hi* magazine's Arabic and English Web sites highlight online forums and question-and-answer sections as well. A sampling of some Web site forum questions: getting a U.S. work visa, reality television shows, drug use among Olympic athletes, robots, eloping, using the Internet to find lost friends, interracial marriage, and art in New York's Chelsea district.

With only a year of publication, it may be too early to pass judgment on *Hi*'s impact and importance. For example, *Span* magazine, published by the U.S. embassy in New Delhi, has become an established name for large numbers of educated Indian readers—but only after decades of publication. Just within the last year *Span* launched new editions in Hindi and Urdu.

Hi's dilemma is not unlike a promising new television show that has not yet found its audience and made a sufficient return on its investment. Detractors point to readerships that do not seem to justify the funding levels. Supporters, optimistic that the potential for a larger audience is out there, plead for more resources and an increased budget for promotion and advertising—two activities deeply antithetical to the State Department's conservative culture.

By breaking out of the confines of narrow policy debates, *Hi* appears to be able to connect with new audiences and younger generations—otherwise untouched by official U.S. government information programs—who are looking for the one thing the jihadists and other extremists cannot offer them: a future. *Hi* cannot be—and should not be—the only channel for reaching this successor generation with ideas and images of America, but it may be a promising start.

The Paradox of Print

In talking about effective ways to reach international audiences, the familiar dichotomy between printed and online information is almost always a false one. Neither handing a press release to a gaggle of reporters nor posting a document on the Internet necessarily means that a public diplomacy officer has addressed any aspect of the three-part mandate to "engage, inform, and influence."

Even in a networked world, the Internet can be equal parts information cornucopia and a channel of delusion and lies. Print publications can be outdated and irrelevant—or a powerful combination of argument, image, and documentation, with a shelf life and veracity that satellite television can only dream of possessing.

The challenge, therefore, is not choosing between print and Web, but using digital technology to integrate information on the basis of the four-R's: right content, right audience, right format—right now.

A dazzling Web site or a glossy print publication is little more than an indulgence if it isn't in the right hands, or before the right pair of eyes, at the right time—which, in today's fast-forward world, means sooner rather than later.

Another way of thinking about the problem is to recognize that, with digital information technologies like the Internet, information is liquid: it can be poured into an infinite number of containers and shapes. From this view, the debate over print versus electronic media is irrelevant. The only important question is: what is the most effective way to shape and transmit the right messages to the right audiences in the Arab and Muslim worlds?

In IIP, for example, an information product that begins as print publication will be adapted as an online document or Web site. Conversely, a set of Web pages may be collected and redesigned as a print publication. In the case of electronic journals, the Internet serves primarily as the means of transmission for articles or entire journals that are typically printed out before they are "consumed" by readers. Every study of the Internet, for example, indicates that users will surf through or even read one or two screens—but if they are moved to read a text of three or more screens, they will almost invariably print out the material.

One reason that IIP has made much greater strides in Web content than in wider print distribution is cost. Web work can be labor-intensive and require skilled professionals, but virtual space is generally cheap real estate. Not so with print. As a result, one of the most critical gaps in State's information efforts is finding more cost-effective, rapid-response ways of distributing printed materials—from Arabic book translations, to illustrated pamphlets, to "wider, deeper, younger" audiences generally, and Arab/Muslim readers in particular.

Whether State opts to reinvent a set of regional printing facilities worldwide, for example, or to contract with local just-in-time digital printers in different countries, the costs will be substantial. The Internet notwithstanding, print remains an unrivaled medium for delivering information with impact, and it is well worth the investment.

Charlotte Beers and Shared Values

Charlotte Beers, advertising executive and former undersecretary for public diplomacy and public affairs, did not conceive of *Hi* magazine. However, in the wake of 9/11, she did secure the funds necessary to launch *Hi*, as well as a number of other publishing initiatives that dealt directly with issues of terrorism (*Living Memories: The Human Toll of Terrorism*) and the broader context of the American image in the Muslim world (*Muslim Life in America*).

Her brief tenure as undersecretary illustrated both the perils and the urgency of finding new approaches for expanded engagement with Arab and Muslim audiences. Beers was confirmed less than a month after the 9/11 attacks and left the position for health reasons in March 2003. During that time, she launched the Shared Values initiative that became a target for criticism from the media, resistance from elements of the State Department, and hostility from a number of Arab governments.

In many ways, *Muslim Life in America* exemplified Beers' effort to expand the audience and shift the focus outside the parameters of policy debate. *Muslim Life*, which is both a Web site and a print publication, is low-key and pictorial in its depiction of family, work, and religious life of Muslim Americans. Along with profiles of individuals and families, for example, the *Muslim Life* Web site offers photo galleries on American mosques, everyday life, Muslim schools, and Ramadan observations. By 2004, more than 350,000 copies of *Muslim Life* had been printed in more than twenty languages, and IIP is planning a traveling exhibit, or paper show, that will be available to posts worldwide. A poster from the Mosques of America feature has also proven popular throughout the Middle East.

Criticism focused primarily on a series of expensive, professionally slick print ads, and one- to two-minute television spots, profiling Muslim Americans and highlighting their freedom to express their faith and culture within the larger context of American society. The ads were first published and broadcast during Ramadan in the fall of 2002, although government-controlled networks in Egypt, Jordan, and Lebanon refused to run them.

In one of the spots, Abdul Hammuda, owner of a Lebanese bakery in Toledo, Ohio, where he makes "the greatest pita bread in the nation," said, "Living the straight path in America, I don't think is hard, because it is a choice you have to make. America is a land of opportunity, of equality. We are happy to live here as Muslims and preserve our faith."

Other print and television spots featured a public school teacher; a journalism student from Indonesia; a paramedic with the New York Fire Department; and Elias Zerhouni, born in Algeria, and now director of the

National Institutes of Health. Several of these profiles are also integrated into *Muslim Life in America.*

There were certainly valid concerns about the TV spots: their cost, lengthy production time, and high profile at a time when political-diplomatic channels were overloaded with Middle East violence, terrorism, military operations in Afghanistan, and a build-up to war in Iraq. Nevertheless, much of the criticism reflected a reflexively negative and defensive attitude toward new or imaginative uses of public diplomacy.

One line of criticism suggested that the spots were unnecessary, if not patronizing, since people around the world, including Arabs and Muslims, were fully aware of America's belief in religious freedom. To the contrary, Beers asserted, educated elites in these countries might be familiar with America's religious pluralism, but polls consistently showed that large numbers of people in the Arab and Muslim worlds did not simply dislike U.S. policies, they believed that America was hostile to Islam and discriminated against Muslims.

A study by two American professors, Alice Kendrick of Southern Methodist University and Jami Fullerton of Oklahoma State University, found that the ads produced real results in changing attitudes. In the summer of 2003, they showed the Shared Values ads to international students enrolled at Regents College in London. According to an abstract of their findings:

> Results revealed that viewing the Shared Values Initiative commercials produced immediate and significant attitude shifts. Overall attitudes toward the U.S. government as well as whether Muslims were treated fairly in the United States improved significantly after the videos were shown.[5]

In Indonesia, the one country where the print and TV ads ran extensively, interviews showed viewers expressing genuine surprise that Muslims in America could worship openly, or that women could wear hejabs in public. Follow-up studies in Indonesia, moreover, indicated that the spots achieved "brand" recognition that would be the envy of any similar ad campaign for commercial products.

And that, perhaps, was the heart of the problem. Despite the fact that the Shared Values spots addressed real misperceptions and myths

---

5. Alice Kendrick and Jami Fullerton, "Advertising as Public Diplomacy: Attitude Change Among International Audiences," *Journal of Advertising Research* 44, no. 3, (Sept. 2004).

about America, they carried a heavy load of baggage about American commercialism and mass media. The paradox of using slick ads to dispel images of slick, superficial America did not escape the commentators. On the other hand, the spectacle of government-run broadcasters in the Middle East, who routinely caricature and demonize the United States, piously refusing to run "government-sponsored" propaganda was rich in irony. What did escape the critics were the other elements of the Shared Values campaign, including expanded exchange programs and publication initiatives.

> THERE WERE CERTAINLY VALID CONCERNS ABOUT THE TV SPOTS. NEVERTHELESS, MUCH OF THE CRITICISM REFLECTED A REFLEXIVELY NEGATIVE AND DEFENSIVE ATTITUDE TOWARD NEW OR IMAGINATIVE USES OF PUBLIC DIPLOMACY.

Beers, an advertising professional, was the first official who could talk sensibly about the connections between public relations and public diplomacy. The idea of "selling" America like a product was nonsense, she insisted; the objective must be to build relationships based on trust, understanding, and mutual concerns—hardly unfamiliar terms to the State Department's public diplomacy officers.

Beers was also insistent and tough minded about heeding the discipline of persuasive communication, whether in printed materials, exchange programs, or mass-media broadcasting: credibility, context, listening, and shared interests. Instead of focusing on the message you are trying to get out, she reiterated, focus on the response you are trying to achieve. In every speech her mantra was the same: "It's not what *you* say that matters, it's what *they* hear."

As an example, Beers pointed to an early test, in November 2001, of anti-terrorism messages displayed on two posters and shown to focus groups in Lebanon. One said: "Terrorism Has No Future: Over 7,000 lives lost to terrorism, 2,000 of them were children." The other: "Terrorism Has No Future: The lifespan of a human being is 68 years. The lifespan of a terrorist is 28 years."

Despite the power and legitimacy of the message, the responses tended to be along the lines: "I see pictures like this every day," and "What one person calls terrorists, another person calls freedom fighters."

The message may have been right, but not the response; the idea was dropped. Instead, Beers pursued the Shared Values idea with a focus on topics that *did* resonate with Arab and Muslim audiences: faith, family, and education.

Adherence to these fundamental principles of communication may, in the end, constitute a more important legacy for Charlotte Beers than whether the Department launches another high-profile advertising campaign for American society and values. Certainly, they constitute a valid set of parameters for assessing the current mix of print and electronic products of the State Department's Bureau of International Information Programs, and determining where resources should flow most effectively in telling America's story to wider, deeper, younger, and more diverse audiences in the Arab and Muslim worlds.

The United States must not cease to explain and defend its policies at every opportunity, to every possible audience, no matter how hostile or unsympathetic. But we also need to shatter the narrow confines of political debate, change the subject, and talk more about a shared future of opportunity and freedom in far different ways with larger and different global audiences.

11. Conclusions and an Action Plan

William A. Rugh

The experts who contributed to this volume demonstrate that U.S. diplomats are forced to confront a formidable public diplomacy crisis in Arab and Muslim nations with scant support from Washington. Public diplomacy professionals do their best to convey U.S. policy with the means available to them, but years of regional neglect and a steady erosion of funding, among other factors, have left them with few effective tools.

To revitalize U.S. engagement with Arab and Muslim nations, we need not develop new tools from scratch. As the previous essays have shown, many public diplomacy mechanisms that proved effective in the past can be reinstated or modified to address current challenges. This chapter will first summarize some basic premises regarding public diplomacy practices aimed at Arab and Muslim audiences. Based on these premises, it will then offer an action plan, which calls for employing specific tools that will greatly improve chances of our success in the region.

Premises
Public diplomacy is a vital instrument of national policy that must be used in a more vigorous and coordinated fashion in the Arab and Muslim worlds, where an intense struggle of ideas is raging. While public diplomacy remains an instrument that is managed and guided by the government, private citizens, who participate in many public diplomacy programs, have been important to its success.

Three major factors, namely increased security measures, decreased funding, and the merger of USIA into the Department of State, have combined to hamper U.S. public diplomacy in Arab and Muslim countries. All three predate 9/11. First, attacks on American facilities abroad put pressure on public affairs officers (PAOs) to restrict access to their libraries and other centers, which had been important venues for discourse. Then, at the end of the Cold War, Americans seemed to lose interest in public diplomacy, and funding declined rapidly. Slashed funding forced reductions in staffing and terminated several programs. Tools of proven effectiveness were abandoned. There has been some recognition in Washington after 9/11 that public diplomacy needs support, but professionals agree that funding levels remain shockingly low relative to the need. National security measures have intensified since 9/11, which has inhibited participation in exchange programs. Finally, many PAOs believe the USIA-State merger has hampered their effectiveness abroad. Many also fear that their

> WE CANNOT CONDUCT PUBLIC DIPLOMACY EFFECTIVELY WHILE HIDING INSIDE FORTRESSES.

expertise has been devalued by the State Department bureaucracy, and the professionalism and flexibility that they enjoyed under USIA has been lost.

A fourth factor, the revolution in communications technology, has presented public diplomatists with an additional challenge because their target audiences have become deluged with information and opinion messages, some of them hostile to the United States, and they must try to be heard in this cacophony.

Public diplomacy must make use of a variety of instruments, and not depend on only one or a few. In this collection of essays, specialists discussed broadcasting, educational exchanges, print media, centers and libraries, and personnel development. An interactive component involving dialogue is often the most powerful device. International broadcasting has made effective use of call-in programs. And the most appealing aspect of the new *Hi* magazine is its interactive component. Formats that encourage mutual exchanges are effective because they can focus on issues of direct concern to our audiences, show respect for their opinions, and facilitate direct, immediate responses to questions. At the same time, long-term instruments such as educational exchanges and English teaching are vital. There is no silver bullet. A carefully orchestrated combination of all appropriate instruments, designed with the audiences in mind, is essential.

Public diplomacy practitioners have taken advantage of new technologies, such as satellite broadcasting, the Internet, and digital video conferencing. They have adapted their craft to the changing environment. However, the latest technology cannot substitute for face-to-face encounters between Americans and their foreign interlocutors. Most public diplomacy professionals regard personal contact and direct communication as an absolutely indispensable ingredient of an effective public diplomacy program. This is especially true in Arab and Muslim countries, where a personal effort can be the most powerful component of a program. Listening carefully is an important component of persuasion, and the best practitioners of public diplomacy are good at both.

Action Plan

To restore effective public diplomacy in Arab and Muslim worlds, we strongly urge the U.S. Administration to implement the following recommendations:

- **Expand public diplomacy in the Arab and Muslim worlds,** where we are engaged in an intense struggle of ideas for the support and understanding of those publics. Public diplomacy is a vital instrument of national policy.

- **Employ a combination of diplomacy instruments** designed with the intended target audience in mind. No single tool or technique alone is sufficient. Strategic and tactical planning must involve professionals with field experience in the Arab and Muslim worlds.

- **Expand the use of local media channels** by officials at embassies and in Washington to increase American participation in the global debate on policies and issues relevant to our audiences. American citizens, such as Arab Americans and Muslim Americans, should also be encouraged to appear in foreign media and in speakers programs abroad.

- **Prepare public affairs officers, their staffs, and other officers at embassies in the Arab and Muslim worlds to proactively engage key audiences in an ongoing dialogue** on U.S. policy and on American society and culture.

- **Revive American centers, English language programs, and libraries overseas.** Any security problems must be solved so these centers can open and thrive once more. We cannot conduct public diplomacy effectively while hiding inside fortresses.

- **Reinvigorate and expand exchange programs.** Student exchanges and speaker and international visitor programs should include current policymakers and opinion leaders, as well as youths and future leaders. These programs benefit the United States. Therefore, reasonable and proportional security measures affecting exchanges must be implemented immediately to minimize barriers that inhibit the flow of visitors between the U.S. and Arab and Muslim countries.

- **Increase the number of public diplomacy officer positions at embassies in Arab and Muslim countries.** The harmful staffing reductions must be reversed.

- **Give PAOs more autonomy to carry out their programs locally,** and provide them more coordinated support from Washington.

- **Increase the number of foreign service officers who specialize in public diplomacy.** Specialization and expertise is crucial to success. The reputation and role of this "cone" should be enhanced so that it is highly respected and career-enhancing. In addition, language skills and cultural awareness must be strengthened with training incentives.
- **Consolidate public diplomacy management within the State Department** to provide PAOs at embassies abroad with clearer backstopping and more coordinated program support, following a carefully constructed strategic and tactical plan designed by public diplomacy experts in the region.
- **Revive The Voice of America Arabic Service.** VOA Arabic, with its varied programming aimed at many types of listeners, would complement Radio Sawa and Alhurra Television, and would reach a wide demographic. All of these services must be technologically upgraded to reach more Arab and Muslim audiences.
- **Translate more American books into Arabic** and other relevant languages, concentrating on basic works that help Arab and Muslim audiences understand American society and culture. We must also seek imaginative ways to deliver written materials, such as electronically.
- To support these essential recommendations, **at a minimum, the United States should quadruple total spending on public diplomacy,** raising the level to at least $4 billion.

Our recommendations are numerous and far-reaching. They may seem costly. On one level, they promote the development and use of particular tools that our diplomacy professionals require to succeed in the field. But our recommendations also aim to address a profound imbalance between America's urgent need for effective public diplomacy and America's inadequate level of commitment to the institution and its professionals. The United States currently spends $1 billion on public diplomacy (including broadcasting). Raising the amount to our suggested $4 billion still leaves public diplomacy funded at merely one percent of our military budget. Our recommendations are more than just correctives that reaffirm public diplomacy's vital role in U.S. foreign policy. The bottom line is that we must improve our relations with Arab and Muslim nations, and these recommendations will help us achieve that end. What will it cost us if we don't?

Contributors

Cresencio Arcos

Cresencio (Cris) Arcos is director of international affairs at the U.S. Department of Homeland Security. Previously, as AT&T's vice president and managing director for international public affairs for Latin America and Canada, he was responsible for engaging foreign governments and the U.S. government on issues such as market access, regulatory framework, business development, and fair competition. He served as a member of the President's Foreign Intelligence Advisory Board at the White House (1999-2003). Mr. Arcos has also served in several positions at the U.S. Information Agency and the U.S. Department of State, retiring with the rank of ambassador after a twenty-five–year career, and he has published several articles on U.S. foreign policy.

Barry Ballow

Barry Ballow left the position of director of the Office of Academic Exchange Programs at the U.S. Department of State in January 2004, after nearly forty-two years of service with the State Department and the U.S. Information Agency. He was a manager of exchange programs within the Bureau of Educational and Cultural Affairs from 1985–2004. His overseas assignments included the Republic of Congo, the Democratic Republic of Congo, Vietnam, Morocco, and Cameroon.

James L. Bullock

James Bullock has been a public affairs officer, the head of a U.S. embassy public affairs/U.S. Information Service operation six times, all in Arab countries: Qatar, Lebanon, Iraq, Tunisia, Morocco, and Egypt. Mr. Bullock left his assignment at the embassy in Morocco during the summer of 1999, just prior to the USIA-State merger, to return to Washington, where he was able to observe for four years the restructuring of U.S. public diplomacy operations from the center. In the summer of 2003, shortly after returning from temporary duty with the U.S. Military Public Affairs Center in Kuwait during our initial military operations in Iraq, he was assigned to take over the public affairs section at the embassy in Cairo.

Howard Cincotta

Howard Cincotta spent more than thirty years as a writer and editor with the U.S. Information Agency and the State Department's Bureau of International Information

Programs. He worked on USIA magazines for Africa and the former Soviet Union, and headed the Agency's Special Publications unit. From 1995 to 2001, he was chief of the Electronic Media office that managed the State Department's overseas Web site. Mr. Cincotta has written recent State Department publications on terrorism, Iraq, and public diplomacy. He has also served as a speechwriter for several State Department officials, including Undersecretary of State Charlotte Beers and Assistant Secretary Patricia Harrison. He now works as a freelance writer.

Barry Fulton

Barry Fulton is a research professor at George Washington University and a consultant on knowledge management at the U.S. Department of State. He sits on the board of directors of the Salzburg Seminar and of InterMedia. He served on the Council on Foreign Relations Task Force on Public Diplomacy and the Defense Science Board Task Force on Managed Information Dissemination. He was executive director of the Center for Strategic and International Studies research on Reinventing Diplomacy in the Information Age. Professor Fulton was director of GWU's Public Diplomacy Institute from 2001 to 2004, and was associate director of USIA from 1994 to 1997. During a thirty-year career with USIA, he served in Brussels, Rome, Tokyo, Karachi, and Islamabad. He established and directed the American Forces Radio and Television Service in Turkey as a lieutenant in the U.S. Air Force.

Alan L. Heil Jr.

Alan L. Heil Jr. is a former deputy director of VOA and author of *Voice of America: A History* (Columbia University Press, 2003). He retired after thirty-six years at the nation's largest publicly funded overseas network, serving in a number of posts there including Middle East correspondent, 1965-1971; chief of News and Current Affairs, 1973-1982; and deputy director of programs, 1987-1994. Mr. Heil has written extensively about international broadcasting and the Middle East, contributing to *Popular Communications*, the *Foreign Service Journal*, the *Monitoring Times*, the *Washington Report on Middle East Affairs*, and the *Channel*, a London-based periodical of the Association for International Broadcasting. He has appeared on NPR, C-SPAN, and the VOA worldwide call-in *Talk to America*.

Kenton W. Keith

Kenton Keith spent thirty-three years in the U.S. foreign service, principally with the U.S. Information Agency. He served as ambassador to the State of Qatar. Previously, he served as a public affairs officer in Cairo and Damascus, senior cultural affairs officer in Paris, deputy PAO in Brasilia, and he held other positions in Saudi Arabia, Morocco, and Iraq. Amb. Keith was also the Near East/South Asia/North Africa Area Director in USIA Washington. He is currently senior vice president at Meridian International Center, Washington, D.C.

Marc Lynch

Marc Lynch, associate professor of political science at Williams College, received his PhD from Cornell University in 1997. He has written widely about Arab public opinion and the Arab media, especially in Jordan, as well as about the potential and problems of international dialogue. His second book, *Iraq and the New Arab Public Sphere*, will be published by Columbia University Press in 2005.

Norman J. Pattiz

Norm Pattiz is a member of the U.S. Broadcasting Board of Governors, appointed by President Clinton in 2000 and repainted by President Bush in 2002. He has been the driving force behind the creation of Radio Sawa and Alhurra Television. Mr. Pattiz is the founder and chairman of Westwood One, Inc., America's largest radio network and a leading supplier of television programming. Westwood One owns or distributes CBS Radio News, CNN Radio News, NBC Radio News, CNBC Business Radio, Marketwatch.com, and Metro Networks. Mr. Pattiz is a regent of the University of California and former president of the Broadcast Education Association. He serves on the board of the Annenberg School of Communication at the University of Southern California and previously served on the board of Rand's Center for Middle East Public Policy. He is a member of the Council of Foreign Relations and the Pacific Council of International Relations.

William A. Rugh

William A. Rugh was a U.S. foreign service officer with the U.S. Information Agency 1964-1995, serving in Washington (he was USIA's Near East/South Asia area director 1989-1992) and at seven Middle Eastern diplomatic posts including as U.S. ambassador to Yemen 1984-1987 and to the United Arab Emirates 1992-1995. He holds a PhD in political science from Columbia University, and he taught as an adjunct professor at the Fletcher School of Law and Diplomacy of Tufts University, 1987-1989. He has published numerous journal articles and op-eds on Middle Eastern subjects. In 2004, Praeger/Greenwood published his book *Arab Mass Media*. Currently he is an associate of Georgetown's Institute for the Study of Diplomacy, an adjunct scholar at the Middle East Institute, a trustee of the American University in Cairo, and a board member at AMIDEAST, where he was president and CEO 1995-2003.

Shibley Telhami

Shibley Telhami is the Anwar Sadat Professor for Peace and Development at the University of Maryland, College Park, and non-resident senior fellow at the Saban Center at the Brookings Institution. Among Professor Telhami's several board and advisory positions, he has served on the U.S. Advisory Group on Public Diplomacy for the Arab and Muslim World, and co-drafted the report of their findings, *Changing Minds, Winning Peace*. He is the author of several books, reports, and articles, including *The Stakes: America and the Middle East* (Westview Press, 2003; updated in 2004), which was selected by *Foreign Affairs* as one of the top five books on the Middle East in 2003.

About the Public Diplomacy Council

The Public Diplomacy Council (PDC) is a non-profit organization committed to the academic study, professional practice, and responsible advocacy of public diplomacy.

PDC members believe that understanding and influencing foreign publics, and dialogue between Americans and the citizens of other countries, are vital to the national interest and the conduct of 21st century diplomacy.

The Public Diplomacy Council was founded in 1988 as the Public Diplomacy Foundation. Dedicated to fostering greater public recognition of public diplomacy in the conduct of foreign affairs, the Foundation evolved to serve also as a resource and advocate for the teaching, training, and development of public diplomacy as an academic discipline.

In 2001, the Foundation joined with The George Washington University School of Media and Public Affairs and Elliott School of International Affairs to establish the Public Diplomacy Institute.

The Foundation changed its name to the Public Diplomacy Council in 2002 and became a membership organization with an elected board of directors. The Council maintains close ties with the USIA Alumni Association, whose president is an *ex officio* member of the Council's board of directors.

Objectives

The Public Diplomacy Council is committed to fostering awareness of the public, social, educational, and cultural dimensions of world affairs. In recent years, the Council and the Public Diplomacy Institute have become a primary source of information on the academic study of public diplomacy and on legislative and executive branch efforts to strengthen its use as an essential element of statecraft.

Assumptions

- Publics and their opinions matter increasingly in a globalizing world.

- U.S. statecraft should rely on careful analysis of the public dimension of issues.
- Informed judgments about global trends depend on an understanding of social and cultural dynamics and public opinion here and abroad.
- Civil society, the arts and educational communities are crucial intermediaries with counterparts in other nations.
- Public Diplomacy budgets, training, and recruitment currently do not reflect the growing importance of public diplomacy.
- Twenty-first century diplomacy will rely increasingly on mastery of modern telecommunications, yet the growth in mass communication creates a more urgent need for interpersonal communication.

Purposes

- Increase understanding of the public dimension of world affairs and of public diplomacy as an essential instrument of statecraft.
- Encourage teaching, research, and writing about public diplomacy.
- Develop and promote high standards in the professional practice of public diplomacy.
- Encourage cooperative relations between the U.S. government and civil society, communications, arts, and educational and cultural institutions.
- Foster dialogue between the government and non-governmental sector about the changing role of publics in a globalizing world and the impact on publics of new communications technologies.
- Build the bases for understanding public diplomacy and public perceptions by supporting the preservation of archival materials.

Funding

The Public Diplomacy Council has no government connection and receives no financial support from any government source. It seeks support from foundation grants and corporate gifts.

The Council is a 501(c)(3) organization that relies on the dues, contributions, and volunteer work of its members. Donations to the Council are tax deductible.

For further information contact:

William P. Kiehl
Executive Director
The Public Diplomacy Council
School of Media and Public Affairs
George Washington University
805 21st Street, NW, Suite 400
Washington, DC 20052
Telephone: (202) 994-0389
E-mail: wpkiehl@earthlink.net
Web site: www.pdi.gwu.edu

Index